THE
CHINA
STUDY
ALL-STAR COLLECTION

THE
CHINA
STUDY
ALL-STAR COLLECTION

WHOLE FOOD, PLANT-BASED RECIPES
FROM YOUR FAVORITE VEGAN CHEFS

EDITED BY LEANNE CAMPBELL, PHD
FOREWORD BY T. COLIN CAMPBELL, COAUTHOR OF *THE CHINA STUDY*

BENBELLA BOOKS, INC.
DALLAS, TX

Recipes are based on the research of T. Colin Campbell as presented in *The China Study* (BenBella Books, 2005), coauthored by T. Colin Campbell, PhD, & Thomas M. Campbell II, MD. References to page numbers in *Whole* are based on the first edition hardcover.

BenBella Books, Inc.
10300 N. Central Expressway
Suite #530
Dallas, TX 75231
www.benbellabooks.com
Send feedback to feedback@benbellabooks.com

Printed in the United States of America
10 9 8 7 6 5 4 3 2

Library of Congress Cataloging-in-Publication Data
  The China study all-star collection : whole food, plant-based recipes from your favorite vegan chefs / edited by LeAnne Campbell, PhD ; introduction by T. Colin Campbell, coauthor of The China study.
      pages   cm
    Includes bibliographical references and index.
    ISBN 978-1-939529-97-8 (hardback)—ISBN 978-1-940363-01-1 (electronic)
    1. Vegetarian cooking.   I. Campbell, LeAnne.
    TX837.C4585   2014
    641.5′636—dc23   2013041459

Editing by LeAnne Campbell
Copyediting by Vy Tran
Proofreading by Brittany Dowdle and James Fraleigh
Index by Jigsaw Information
Text design by Kit Sweeney
Text composition by Ralph Fowler
Cover design by Bradford Foltz
Jacket design by Sarah Dombrowsky
Printed by Versa Press, Inc.

Distributed by Perseus Distribution
www.perseusdistribution.com

To place orders through Perseus Distribution:
Tel: 800-343-4499
Fax: 800-351-5073
E-mail: orderentry@perseusbooks.com

Significant discounts for bulk sales are available. Please contact Glenn Yeffeth at glenn@benbellabooks.com or 214-750-3628.

24

28

38

52

56

CONTENTS

SIDE DISHES

242

255

263

269

273

FOREWORD

In many ways, the world has changed dramatically since *The China Study* was released in 2005. Ten years ago, most doctors thought the idea that diet might solve serious health problems was fantasy. Now I hear of more and more doctors actually recommending a plant-based diet to their patients!

Ten years ago, plant-based eating was considered the province of the radical fringe and was viewed as dangerous and unhealthy. Now mainstream *New York Times* food critic Mark Bittman has released a book entitled *VB6: Eat Vegan Before 6:00 to Lose Weight and Restore Your Health . . . for Good*, which quickly became a best-seller. And former President of the United States Bill Clinton announced that his plant-based diet (inspired, in part, by *The China Study*) has allowed him to overcome heart disease! James Cameron, producer of *Titanic* and *Avatar* and record holder of going to the greatest depth in the ocean, said that he and his family made a change almost overnight after viewing the film *Forks Over Knives* and reading *The China Study*. So, too, did many world-class athletes, like golfer Gary Player, footballer Tony Gonzalez, champion Ultimate Fighter James Wilks, and world record holder strongman Patrik Baboumian.

My coauthor, Dr. Tom Campbell, and I have sold well over one million copies of *The China Study*, and we're proud of the role we have played in this transformation. Our work, and that of writers and researchers such as Dr. John McDougall, Dr. Caldwell B. Esselstyn, Dr. Dean Ornish, Dr. Neal Barnard, Dr. Pamela Popper, and others, have made major contributions in shifting public opinion in this direction.

But we're just at the beginning. America's health is still failing miserably. We spend far more, per capita, on health care than any other society in the world, and yet two-thirds of Americans are overweight, and the epidemics of diabetes, heart disease, and cancer continue unabated. Our elected officials spend their time fighting bitterly over alternative health care proposals—none of which address the fundamental problems that could lead to less demand for health care services.

The solution is quite simple, though. A good diet is the most powerful weapon we have in the fight for real health. As we said in *The China Study*, the solution comes down to three things: breakfast, lunch, and dinner.

In over five decades of biomedical research, my research group and I have learned, in so many ways, that a whole food, plant-based diet promotes optimal health and the prevention and even reversal in many cases of heart disease, diabetes, obesity, cancer, autoimmune diseases, and brain disorders.

I've received overwhelming feedback from people who have seen incredible health results after transitioning to a whole food, plant-based diet. But I'm still often asked about some of the more practical, everyday aspects of adopting and living this lifestyle. Perhaps the most common question is simply, "What do I eat?" My daughter, Dr. LeAnne Campbell, released a compilation of some of our family's favorite recipes in her best-seller, *The China Study Cookbook*. That book is the closest representation of what my family and I eat.

In this follow-up, LeAnne has gathered some of the most popular and influential plant-based chefs to share their best dishes, all following the nutrition principles laid out in *The China Study*. Joining LeAnne for *The China Study All-Star Collection* is a diverse list of contributors: Chef AJ, Ani Phyo, Christina Ross, Christy Morgan, Del Sroufe, Dreena Burton, Heather Crosby, John and Mary McDougall, Laura Theodore, Lindsay Nixon, and Tracy Russell. Whether you've been living plant-based for decades or you are just beginning, I think you will find this a useful source of tasty, healthful recipes.

Today, more than one-third of American children either are or are in danger of becoming overweight, forecasting future personal health problems and suggesting an alarming statistic on the future health of our country. But pioneering chefs like those contributing to this book continue to demonstrate the ease and pleasure of using a plant-based diet, and I see increasing promise that our society will wake up and embrace this proven approach to optimal health. The rewards go far beyond regaining personal health; indeed, this way of eating results in societal, environmental, and even planetary benefits of gigantic proportions.

—T. COLIN CAMPBELL, PHD
Coauthor of the bestselling *The China Study*, Professor Emeritus of Nutritional Biochemistry, Cornell University

THE RECIPES

BREADS

&

MUFFINS

APPLE-SWIRL LOAF

MAKES 1 LOAF RECIPE BY DREENA BURTON

This quick bread is easy to make but looks very impressive with its apple-cinnamon swirled effect! The aroma during baking is divine, too.

FOR THE APPLE MIXTURE
½ cup peeled and diced apple
1 teaspoon fresh lemon juice
¼ cup unsweetened applesauce
3 tablespoons coconut sugar or other
    unrefined sugar
1 teaspoon ground cinnamon
⅛ teaspoon ground allspice

FOR THE BATTER
1½ cups whole-wheat pastry flour (or 1⅔ cups
    whole-grain spelt flour for a wheat-free
    option)
½ cup oat flour
1½ teaspoons baking powder
½ teaspoon baking soda
½ teaspoon ground cinnamon
¼ teaspoon sea salt
¾ cup plain nondairy milk
½ cup maple syrup
1½ teaspoons vanilla extract
1 teaspoon fresh lemon juice or apple cider
    vinegar

1. Preheat oven to 350°F and then prepare your loaf dish: Using a paper towel, wipe a smidgen of oil around the inside of a 9 × 5 glass loaf dish and then line with a strip of parchment paper (or use a silicone dish).

2. In a bowl, toss apples with lemon juice and then add applesauce, sugar, cinnamon, and allspice. Mix and set aside.

3. In a large bowl, combine dry ingredients for batter, sifting in baking powder and soda. Mix well.

4. In a small bowl, combine milk, maple syrup, vanilla, and lemon juice. Add wet mixture to dry, stirring through until just well combined without overmixing.

5. Add about three-fourths of the apple mixture to batter and, using a spoon or knife, ever so slightly fold or swirl it into the batter. It's okay to have thicker spots; these will create delicious flavor swirls.

6. Transfer batter into loaf pan and dollop the remaining apple mixture on top.

7. Bake for 35–45 minutes until golden and a toothpick or skewer inserted in the center comes out clean. Remove from oven, keep in glass dish, and transfer to a cooling rack until completely cool. Once cool, remove loaf and cut into slices.

MOM'S BANANA BREAD

MAKES 1 LOAF

RECIPE BY JOHN AND MARY MCDOUGALL

2¼ cups whole-wheat flour
1 teaspoon baking soda
1 teaspoon baking powder
4 ripe bananas

1 12-ounce can frozen apple juice concentrate, thawed
3 teaspoons Egg Replacer (see Tip) mixed with 6 tablespoons water

1. Preheat oven to 350°F.
2. Mix dry ingredients together.
3. Mash bananas and mix with apple juice concentrate and the Egg Replacer and water.
4. Combine wet and dry ingredients and beat with whisk until blended.
5. Pour into a nonstick, standard-size loaf pan. Bake for 60 minutes.

TIP

Egg Replacer is made by EnerG Foods and can be found in most natural food stores.

DIETARY FIBER AND THE IMPORTANCE OF WHOLE FOODS

Did you know about the benefits of dietary fiber? As T. Colin Campbell stated in *The Low-Carb Fraud*, "Whole foods that contain dietary fiber, in its many complex forms, *are* associated with lower incidence of colon cancer, lower blood cholesterol, and lower breast cancer—inducing estrogen levels."

*The Low-Carb Fraud, p. 19

CORN BREAD

I love corn bread with soup or chili for lunch or dinner, or even with some apple butter on it for a quick breakfast.

1½ cups whole-wheat pastry flour
1½ cups cornmeal
4 teaspoons baking powder
½ teaspoon sea salt

2 tablespoons Best Date Syrup Ever (p. 51)
½ cup unsweetened applesauce
2 cups unsweetened almond milk

1. Preheat oven to 350°F.
2. In a medium bowl, combine the flour, cornmeal, baking powder, and salt.
3. Make a well in the center of the flour mixture by scooping the flour to the side of the bowl with a spoon, and add the date syrup, applesauce, and almond milk to the well. Then gently fold the liquid mixture into the flour mixture.
4. Spoon the batter into an 8 × 8 nonstick baking dish and bake for 30–35 minutes until a toothpick inserted in the center of the pan comes out clean. Let cool before serving.

VARIATION

BLUEBERRY-CORNBREAD MUFFINS

Add ½ pint fresh blueberries to the batter and bake in nonstick muffin tins for 25–30 minutes for a nice treat.

> **TIP**
>
> Applesauce is a good substitute for eggs and oil in baking—and you won't taste it.

QUINOA CORN BREAD

MAKES 8 SERVINGS 　　　　　　　　　　　　　　　　　RECIPE BY JOHN AND MARY MCDOUGALL

1 cup water
½ cup dry quinoa
1 cup cornmeal
½ cup whole-wheat flour
1 tablespoon baking powder
1 teaspoon baking soda
½ teaspoon sea salt

1 ear corn, cut off the cob (about ½ cup)
½ ripe banana
¾ cup soy milk
¼ cup maple syrup or agave nectar
3 teaspoons Egg Replacer (see Tip on p. 18)
　　and 4 tablespoons warm water, whisked
　　together until frothy

1. Boil water, add in the dry quinoa, reduce to a simmer, and cover and cook for 15–20 minutes until the water is gone and the quinoa is puffed up. Set aside while preparing the remaining ingredients.

2. In a bowl, combine the cornmeal, flour, baking powder, baking soda, and salt, followed by the corn kernels.

3. In another bowl, mash the banana well, then add in the milk, maple syrup or agave, and Egg Replacer mixture.

4. Combine wet and dry ingredients.

5. Fold in the cooked quinoa. The mixture will be somewhat thick.

6. Spread into a prepared 8 × 8 pan and bake at 350°F for 25–30 minutes. Let cool for 10 minutes before cutting.

BLUEBERRY LASSY MUFFINS SEE PICTURE ON PAGE 13

MAKES 10–12 MUFFINS   RECIPE BY DREENA BURTON

"Lassy" is an affectionate term for molasses in Newfoundland, where I grew up. These lassy muffins combine warm, fragrant spices with plump, juicy blueberries in a tender batter—perfect treat with tea or a cup of vanilla almond milk!

2¼ cups whole-grain spelt flour
¼ cup coconut sugar or other unrefined sugar
2 teaspoons baking powder
½ teaspoon baking soda
¼ teaspoon sea salt
1 teaspoon ground cinnamon
½ teaspoon ground allspice

¼ teaspoon ground ginger
2 tablespoons blackstrap molasses
½ cup unsweetened applesauce
⅓ cup maple syrup
¾ cup plain nondairy milk
1 teaspoon vanilla extract
⅔–¾ cup blueberries (see Tip)

1. Preheat oven to 350°F.

2. In a large bowl, combine the dry ingredients, sifting in the baking powder and baking soda. Stir through until well combined.

3. In another bowl, first combine the molasses with the applesauce and then whisk or stir in the maple syrup, nondairy milk, and vanilla, and mix together.

4. Add the wet mixture to the dry mixture and gently fold and mix through until just combined (do not overmix), finishing with folding in the berries.

5. Spoon the mixture into a muffin pan lined with cupcake liners (this will fill 10–12 muffins nicely).

6. Bake for 22–24 minutes (smaller muffins need less time and berries may affect baking time; see Tip) until a toothpick inserted in the center comes out clean.

> **TIP**
>
> If using large frozen blueberries, you may need to bake for another minute or two since they take longer to cook through. If using small frozen blueberries, bake for about 22–23 minutes (a little longer if you're making just 10 large muffins).

JUST BANANAS BLUEBERRY MUFFINS

MAKES 12 MUFFINS   RECIPE BY CHEF AJ

4 cups oat flour
1 tablespoon baking powder
1 teaspoon baking soda
2 teaspoons ground cinnamon
8 ripe bananas

1 cup unsweetened apple juice
1 cup unsweetened applesauce
1 tablespoon apple cider vinegar
1 tablespoon vanilla extract
2 cups frozen blueberries

1. Preheat oven to 350°F.

2. Place flour in a large bowl and add all the other dry ingredients.

3. Puree bananas in a food processor until smooth. Add the apple juice, applesauce, apple cider vinegar, and vanilla, and process again until combined.

4. Pour blended mixture over dry ingredients and mix until just combined. Do not overmix. Gently fold in blueberries.

5. Pour into muffin liners, filling each about two-thirds full. Bake for 40–45 minutes until a toothpick inserted in the center comes out clean.

ZUCCHINI & SUMMER SQUASH MUFFINS

MAKES 12 MUFFINS   RECIPE BY HEATHER CROSBY

A gluten-free, nondairy twist on zucchini muffins that will have everyone asking for seconds.

FOR THE DRY INGREDIENTS
¾ cup almond flour
1 cup sweet sorghum flour
½ cup Sucanat
1 teaspoon baking soda
1 teaspoon baking powder
1 teaspoon ground cinnamon
¼ teaspoon ground cardamom
¼ teaspoon ground sea salt

FOR THE WET INGREDIENTS
1 tablespoon chia seeds
1 cup warm water
2 teaspoons apple cider vinegar
1 teaspoon vanilla extract

FOR THE FOLD-INS
¾ cup shredded zucchini
¾ cup shredded summer squash
¼ cup chopped pecans
½ cup chopped walnuts

1. Preheat oven to 350°F.
2. Using a grater or food processor, shred zucchini and summer squash. Place onto a clean cloth towel and sprinkle veggies with a teeny pinch of salt. After 2 minutes, cover, roll up, and press to remove excess water from veggies. Set aside.
3. Sift dry ingredients together into a large bowl.
4. Place wet ingredients into the blender but let them sit for 5 minutes so chia can plump. After 5 minutes, blend until smooth.
5. Place liners into cupcake tins.
6. Mix together wet and dry ingredients. Fold in zucchini, squash, and nuts.
7. Quickly spoon batter into liners until they are full and place in oven.
8. Bake for 25 minutes. Remove from oven and allow muffins to cool in the tin.

If you can't find unbleached parchment liners, simply cut twelve 4 × 4 squares of unbleached parchment paper. Press into muffin compartment to create homemade tulip liners—filling them with batter will help them stay in place.

With gluten-free, nondairy baking, it's very important to keep the wet and dry ingredients separate until you are ready to bake. Once mixed, a chemical reaction begins between leavening ingredients and acids to "fluff" the batter. When your muffin tins are lined, the oven is preheated, and you have a spoon ready and a silicone spatula on-hand for folding, *then* you are ready to mix up wet and dry ingredients. Once muffins are in the oven, do not open the oven door until the timer goes off. This kind of baking is sensitive and it's important to keep the temperature consistent.

Try baking muffins in mini muffin tins for bite-size goodies. Just adjust the baking time to 15 minutes.

For extra flavor, toast pecans and walnuts for 5–7 minutes in an oven heated to 350°F before folding into batter.

BREAKFAST DISHES

MIXED BERRY COUSCOUS SURPRISE | 36

GINGERBREAD GRANOLA

MAKES ABOUT 4½ CUPS   RECIPE BY DREENA BURTON

Bring the beauty and aroma of freshly baked gingerbread into a granola that is perfect for breakfast, snacking—or for gifting during the holidays!

3 cups rolled oats
⅓–½ cup chopped pecans or ¼ cup hemp seeds (see Tips)
1½ teaspoons ground cinnamon
¾–1 teaspoon ground ginger
¾ teaspoon ground allspice
⅛ teaspoon ground cloves
¼ teaspoon sea salt

3 tablespoons cashew butter or almond butter
3–4 tablespoons maple syrup, more or less to taste
½ tablespoon blackstrap molasses
¼ cup brown rice syrup
1 teaspoon vanilla extract (optional)
¼ cup dried cranberries or other dried fruit (optional, see Tips)

1. Preheat oven to 300°F and line a large rimmed baking sheet with parchment paper.

2. In a large bowl, combine the oats, pecans or hemp seeds, spices, and salt.

3. In another bowl, first combine the nut butter with the maple syrup and molasses, stirring to fully blend. Add the brown rice syrup and vanilla and stir through.

4. Transfer mixture to the lined baking sheet and spread out to evenly distribute. Bake for 27–30 minutes, stirring a couple of times throughout baking to ensure the mixture browns evenly.

5. Remove from oven, stir in dried fruit if desired, and bake for just another 2–3 minutes.

6. Remove from oven and let cool completely. Once cooled, store in an airtight container. Eat straight, with nondairy milk, or top with fresh fruit or nondairy yogurt.

TIPS

If you like, substitute 3–4 tablespoons pumpkin seeds or sunflower seeds in place of the nuts or hemp seeds.

Try adding a few tablespoons of finely chopped crystallized ginger instead of cranberries or raisins. It will add a definite flavor kick!

ORANGE & PEPITA GRANOLA

MAKES 10+ SERVINGS   RECIPE BY HEATHER CROSBY

Anyone who grew up eating boxed, processed cereal remembers how fruity and delicious the milk tasted when you got to the bottom of your bowl. Well, bottoms up! This nutritious granola has the same nostalgic taste without the harmful chemicals, dyes, and flavorings. It also doubles as a tasty snack that travels well.

FOR THE DRY INGREDIENTS
3 cups raw, rolled oats (use gluten-free if you
    have a sensitivity)
1 cup shredded or flaked coconut
1 cup raw pepitas (aka pumpkin seeds)
1 cup raw almonds, roughly chopped
2 navel oranges, zested
1 teaspoon fine ground sea salt

FOR THE WET INGREDIENTS
3 tablespoons fresh orange juice
¾ cup maple syrup
1 teaspoon vanilla extract

1. Preheat oven to 300°F.
2. In a small bowl, stir together wet ingredients.
3. In a large bowl, toss together dry ingredients.
4. Add wet ingredients to dry and fold well.
5. Line 1 or 2 baking sheets with parchment paper—you can split the batch, baking half at a time.
6. Bake the granola for 20–25 minutes.
7. Remove from oven and repeat if you are splitting your batch.
8. Serve with nondairy milk, over chia pudding, or enjoy plain.

> **TIP**
>
> Don't overcrowd your baking sheet—you want the granola evenly spread across the sheet about ¼-inch tall. Overcrowding leads to uneven toasting. If you bake and the edges of granola are browned but the center is not, you may have overcrowded the pan. Simply remove the toasted granola, spread the untoasted around the pan, and bake for longer. Store granola in an airtight glass container in a cool, dark place.

PUMPKIN SEED AND CHOCOLATE CHIP OATMEAL BREAKFAST BARS

MAKES 12–16 BARS   RECIPE BY DREENA BURTON

These are a terrific "on-the-go" healthy breakfast or a perfect snack anytime of the day. Our whole family loves them!

1½ cups rolled oats
1¼ cups oat flour
3–4 tablespoons pumpkin seeds
2–3 tablespoons nondairy chocolate chips
   (see Tip)
1 teaspoon ground cinnamon

⅛–¼ teaspoon freshly grated nutmeg
¼ teaspoon sea salt
⅓ cup brown rice syrup
1–2 tablespoons maple syrup
¼ cup and 2 tablespoons unsweetened plain
   nondairy milk

1. Preheat oven to 350°F.

2. In a large bowl, combine the rolled oats, oat flour, pumpkin seeds, chocolate chips, cinnamon, nutmeg, and salt.

3. In a smaller bowl, combine the brown rice syrup with maple syrup and milk.

4. Add the wet ingredients into the dry mixture, stirring until well combined.

5. Transfer the mixture to an 8 × 8 baking dish or brownie pan lined with parchment paper and press it down until evenly distributed.

6. Using a sharp knife, cut to mark out the bars before you bake them to make it easier to fully cut and remove the bars once baked. (I usually mark out 16 bars, but you can make them whatever size you like.)

7. Bake for 20 minutes, then remove and let cool in pan. Once cooled, use a sharp knife to fully cut the bars, then remove with a spatula.

TIP

Mini chocolate chips are great if you have them. You can also substitute the pumpkin seeds and chocolate chips with raisins, cranberries, sunflower seeds, hemp seeds, unsweetened coconut, or other dried fruit (chopped, if needed).

SWEET POTATO BEGINNINGS

MAKES 2 SERVINGS

RECIPE BY JOHN AND MARY MCDOUGALL

This is a great way to use any leftover yams or sweet potatoes that you have already baked a day or two before. A delicious, sweet, and hearty start for your day!

2 baked yams or sweet potatoes
2 bananas, peeled and sliced

1 apple, cored and chopped
½ teaspoon ground cinnamon

1. Peel and chop the baked yams or sweet potatoes.
2. Combine with the bananas and apples.
3. Mix in the cinnamon.
4. Heat briefly in a microwave oven. Serve warm.

TIPS

Yams and sweet potatoes may be used interchangeably in this (and most other) recipes. These root vegetables are sold most of the year in your markets. Sweet potatoes usually are less moist with a pale orange skin and flesh, and the root vegetables usually sold as yams have a reddish skin and deep orange-colored flesh. Yams are usually very moist.

This recipe may also be served cold or at room temperature.

MIXED BERRY COUSCOUS SURPRISE SEE PICTURE ON PAGE 27

MAKES 5–6 SERVINGS   RECIPE BY CHRISTY MORGAN

This dish is kid-friendly and adults will love it too! It's a great alternative to breakfast cereal, or you could even serve it as a dessert if you add a bit of maple syrup.

2 cups whole-wheat couscous
1½ cups apple juice
1 cup water
1 tablespoon fresh mint, chopped finely
1 cup strawberries, washed and sliced

½ cup raspberries, washed
½ cup blueberries, washed
1–2 teaspoons ground cinnamon
Fresh mint leaves

1. Place couscous in a bowl.

2. Mix together apple juice and water in a saucepan and bring to a boil.

3. Pour liquid over couscous. Cover bowl with a towel or sushi mat and leave for about 5 minutes or until all the liquid is absorbed.

4. Fluff couscous with a fork, then gently stir in mint, berries, and cinnamon.

5. Toss gently. Place in bowls and garnish with mint leaves.

CINNAMON RAISIN FLAX MEAL

MAKES 2 SERVINGS

Energizing and full of fiber and sweetness, this will surely become a regular breakfast staple in your home.

2 Fuji apples
½ cup flax meal
¼ cup raisins
½ teaspoon ground cinnamon

¼ teaspoon vanilla bean
1 cup almond milk
1 banana, sliced
¼ cup pecan pieces

1. Chop the apples into small cubes, leaving the skin on.
2. Add the apples, flax meal, raisins, cinnamon, and vanilla bean to your food processor or blender and process until all ingredients are mixed together. Finished texture should resemble a fine oatmeal.
3. Scoop the mixture into a serving bowl and then add milk, banana, and pecans.

> **TIP**
>
> Try adding in your favorite nuts and seed or different nondairy milks. You can also switch out the apples for pears or bananas.

BLUEBERRY PIE CHIA PARFAIT

MAKES 2–4 SERVINGS   RECIPE BY HEATHER CROSBY

Juicy blueberry compote, almond pie crust crumble, and creamy chia pudding are a magical combination for dessert or, ahem, breakfast.

½ cup chia seeds

FOR THE ALMOND CREAM
2 cups water
1 tablespoon almond butter
1 tablespoon maple syrup
¼ teaspoon vanilla extract
½ teaspoon ground cardamom
Pinch of fine ground sea salt

FOR THE ALMOND PIE CRUST CRUMBLE
1 cup almond flour
3 tablespoons warm water
¼ teaspoon sea salt

FOR THE BLUEBERRY COMPOTE
1 cup fresh blueberries
1 tablespoon maple syrup
2 tablespoons water
½ teaspoon fresh lemon juice
¼ teaspoon fresh thyme leaves, roughly chopped (optional)

1. Preheat oven to 350°F.

2. Place chia seeds in a large glass bowl.

3. Blend together almond cream ingredients until smooth and pour into bowl with chia. Stir well.

4. Cover chia mixture with a clean towel or lid and allow to stand for 15 minutes—chia seeds will plump into pudding.

5. In another glass bowl, mix together pie crust crumble using a fork.

6. Sprinkle crumble evenly onto a baking sheet lined with parchment paper and bake for 5–7 minutes.

7. Remove from oven, shuffle crumble with a fork, and allow to cool on the baking sheet.

8. In a medium saucepan, add all blueberry compote ingredients and warm over medium-high heat. Stir often for about 10 minutes until berries start to break apart. Remove from heat.

9. Layer ingredients into parfait cups and serve warm, room temperature, or chilled—all are delicious.

TIPS

Try using cashew butter as a substitute for almond butter.

Instead of water, almond butter, and maple syrup, simply stir vanilla, cardamom, and a pinch of sea salt into Thai coconut milk for a creamy, rich, and naturally sweet variation of almond cream.

Follow the compote steps to create a variety of fruit compotes. Try peach, mixed berries, fig, or apple for different "pie" fillings for the chia parfait.

Store in airtight glass containers in the fridge for up to one week.

OVERNIGHT MUESLI

MAKES 1 SERVING   RECIPE BY CHEF AJ

Did you know that muesli was introduced around 1900 by the Swiss physician Maximilian Bircher-Benner for patients in his hospital, where a diet rich in fresh fruit and vegetables was an essential part of therapy? Muesli in its modern form became popular in Western countries starting in the 1960s as part of increased interest in health food and vegetarian diets. Traditional muesli was eaten with orange juice and not milk.

¼ cup unsweetened apple juice
¼ cup unsweetened almond milk
½ teaspoon vanilla extract
½ teaspoon apple pie spice or roasted cinnamon

1 tablespoon chia seeds
½ cup gluten-free oats
2 tablespoons currants
1 apple, grated (I prefer Gala)

1. Pour the apple juice and almond milk in a large glass and stir in the vanilla, apple pie spice or cinnamon, and chia seeds.

2. Place the oats and currants in a medium bowl.

3. Grate the apple over the oats.

4. Pour the liquid mixture over the apple and oats and mix well.

5. Place the bowl in the refrigerator covered overnight. The chia seeds will swell and become gelatinous and the next day will have absorbed all of the liquid and become almost like a pudding.

6. In the morning you can enjoy this dish cold or warm it in the microwave. You can also add additional fruits and almond milk, if desired.

BAKED BREAKFAST COOKIES

Scoop ⅓ cup muesli for each cookie, place on a nonstick baking sheet, and bake at 350°F for 30 minutes until golden brown.

> **TIPS**
>
> Both apple pie spice (a blend of cinnamon, nutmeg, and mace) and roasted cinnamon are available at grocery stores like Ralphs and Kroger. Feel free to substitute regular ground cinnamon.
>
> Try substituting grated pear for the apple and goji berries or unsweetened cranberries for the currants.
>
> Dehydrated, this recipe makes an awesome low-fat granola!

CORN PORRIDGE

MAKES 4 SERVINGS   RECIPE BY LEANNE CAMPBELL

3 cups unsweetened almond milk

3 tablespoons raw sugar

1 teaspoon vanilla extract

½ teaspoon ground cinnamon

1 teaspoon grated lemon peel

¾ cup cornmeal

1 cup fresh fruit, sliced (strawberries, blueberries, or bananas)

1. Mix milk, sugar, vanilla, cinnamon, lemon peel, and cornmeal in a saucepan.
2. Bring to a boil and stir for 2–3 minutes until slightly thick.
3. Place sliced fruit in separate bowls, add corn porridge, and serve immediately.

FRESH CORN AND ZUCCHINI FRITTATA

MAKES 5–7 SERVINGS

RECIPE BY CHRISTY MORGAN

When I went vegan, two things I really missed were frittata and quiche. Thankfully, I created this tofu version that is very reminiscent of the egg-based frittatas I used to have.

3 ears corn, cut off the cob (about 1½ cups)
1 medium zucchini, grated
1 14-ounce package extra-firm tofu
3 tablespoons yellow cornmeal
Pinch of sea salt and black pepper
½ teaspoon baking powder

⅓ cup nutritional yeast
1 tablespoon soy sauce or tamari
1 teaspoon maple syrup
2 tablespoons umeboshi vinegar or sherry
  vinegar

1. Preheat oven to 350°F.
2. Place veggies in a large bowl.
3. Combine all remaining ingredients in a food processor. Blend until smooth and no tofu chunks are visible. Be sure to scrape the edges of the bowl a few times to incorporate all the ingredients.
4. Place tofu mixture in bowl with veggies. Fold in the vegetables until well incorporated.
5. Fill a lightly oiled 9-inch round pie pan with mixture and press evenly into pan, smoothing over the top.
6. Bake for 50 minutes uncovered.

TIP

Feel free to change up the vegetables for a slightly different flavor.

TEX-MEX BREAKFAST BOWL

MAKES 6–8 SERVINGS  RECIPE BY LEANNE CAMPBELL

Fiesta Corn Bread from *The China Study Cookbook* (p. 44) or your favorite corn bread recipe
Quick Curried Potatoes (p. 212)

2 cups cooked black beans
1 jar salsa
1 avocado, diced

1. Cook Fiesta Corn Bread and Quick Curried Potatoes.

2. For each serving, assemble the bowl as following: First place a slice of cut corn bread on the bottom of the bowl. Top with 3 large heaping tablespoons of curried potatoes, then 3 tablespoons black beans. Add 3 tablespoons salsa and diced avocado.

3. Serve immediately.

ALMOND CARDAMOM CREAM CHIA PUDDING WITH FRESH BERRIES

MAKES 2–4 SERVINGS

RECIPE BY HEATHER CROSBY

This recipe is a staple in my kitchen—it's easy to prepare, full of beneficial nutrients, and can be adapted with all sorts of fresh fruits, nuts, seeds, and other goodies. Try it for breakfast, as a snack, or as dessert.

½ cup chia seeds

FOR THE CARDAMOM CREAM
2 cups water
1 tablespoon unsalted almond or cashew butter
8 Deglet Noor dates or 5 Medjool dates
¼ teaspoon vanilla extract
½ teaspoon ground cardamom
Pinch of fine ground sea salt

FOR THE TOPPINGS
1 cup fresh berries
Unsulfured shredded or flaked coconut
Hemp seeds

1. Place chia seeds in a large glass bowl.
2. Blend together cardamom cream ingredients until smooth and pour into bowl with chia. Stir well.
3. Cover chia mixture with a clean towel or lid and allow to stand for 15 minutes—chia seeds will plump into pudding.
4. Toast coconut in a dry skillet over medium heat. Stir constantly for 3–5 minutes until lightly browned.
5. Once pudding is set, stir, spoon into a bowl, and top with fresh berries, coconut, and hemp seeds.

TIPS

You can use maple syrup or Sucanat to sweeten instead of dates. Chia pudding is also delicious without sweetener.

Instead of water, almond butter, and dates, simply stir vanilla, cardamom, and a pinch of sea salt into Thai coconut milk for a creamy, rich, and naturally sweet variation of cardamom cream.

Store leftover pudding in an airtight glass container in the fridge for up to one week.

CREAMY BREAKFAST RICE PUDDING

MAKES 2½–3 CUPS RECIPE BY DREENA BURTON

With leftover brown rice, you can have an almost "instant" rice pudding that is a beautiful treat in the morning and a welcome change from oatmeal.

2 cups cooked brown rice, loosely packed, divided
¾–1 cup nondairy milk, divided (see Tips)
1 ripe banana, sliced (about ½–¾ cup) or 1–2 tablespoons maple syrup, coconut sugar, or chopped dried fruits (see Tips)

¼–½ teaspoon ground cinnamon
Few pinches of ground nutmeg
⅛ teaspoon sea salt
Grated orange or lemon zest (optional)

1. In a small saucepan, add 1½ cups cooked rice and the remaining ingredients starting with ¾ cup milk (omit banana if you prefer; see Tips), except for the optional zest.

2. Puree the mixture using a hand blender. Alternatively, you can puree in a blender before adding to the saucepan, but I find the hand blender is quicker and easier for cleanup!

3. Add the remaining ½ cup rice and turn heat to medium-low. Let the mixture thicken and warm for several minutes.

4. Add the remaining milk, if desired, to thin. Taste and adjust with sweetener and orange or lemon zest, if desired, and stir through add-ins if you like!

VARIATIONS

CREAMY CHOCOLATE BREAKFAST RICE PUDDING

Make this pudding chocolatey with the addition of 1–2 tablespoons cocoa powder. You will need extra sweetener to balance the bitterness of the cocoa, so adjust to taste.

ADD-INS

Try adding in a few tablespoons of hemp seeds, 1 tablespoon ground chia seeds, 1–2 tablespoons nut or seed butter (e.g., cashew, almond, pistachio, sunflower), 2–3 tablespoons almond meal, a sprinkle of dried fruit (e.g., chopped dates, goji berries, raisins, dried blueberries, etc.), or some fresh fruit (e.g,. chopped apples or pears in the winter, fresh berries in spring or summer).

The banana adds natural sweetness, so if using, you may not need the maple syrup or coconut sugar—it's up to you. However, note that adding a banana will turn the mixture a darker color with the banana oxidizing and being cooked, so it's best to eat straight away rather than save leftovers. If you don't use the banana, try adding a touch of maple syrup or coconut sugar, or you can add chopped dates or other dried fruits to sweeten.

If using vanilla-flavored nondairy milk, you may not need any additional sweetener. If using an unsweetened variety, you will probably want to bump up the sweetness with the pureed banana or other options.

THE BEST DATE SYRUP EVER

MAKES 3 CUPS

RECIPE BY DEL SROUFE

Dates are nature's candy and a great natural sweetener. Medjool dates are sweeter than other dates, and stevia gives this recipe extra sweetening power, so I can use less of this calorie-dense treat. Use this date syrup as a sweetener in place of your regular sugar.

2 cups pitted Medjool dates
½ teaspoon stevia powder
1½–2 cups water

1. Place all ingredients in a blender and puree until smooth and creamy. Add water as needed to get the mixture to blend.

2. Store refrigerated for up to one week.

OATMEAL WITH POACHED RHUBARB

MAKES 6 SERVINGS RECIPE BY DEL SROUFE

I love to make this dish on weekends in the spring when rhubarb is in season.

1½ pounds rhubarb, peeled if necessary, and
    cut into 3- or 4-inch stalks
¼ cup water
1½ cups Best Date Syrup Ever (p. 51) or more
    to taste

Dash of sea salt
6 servings cooked oatmeal

1. Combine the rhubarb and water in a medium saucepan and bring to a boil over medium heat.

2. Let the mixture simmer for 5 minutes, then add the date syrup and salt.

3. Cook, covered, for 8–10 minutes, until the rhubarb is tender.

4. Puree in a blender with a tight-fitting lid, covered with a towel over the lid (to keep the hot liquid from splattering).

5. Spoon rhubarb into a bowl, place oatmeal in the center, and serve.

QUICK STEEL-CUT OATS WITH BLUEBERRY TOPPING

MAKES 2 SERVINGS   RECIPE BY JOHN AND MARY MCDOUGALL

Steel-cut oats are a very healthy and delicious breakfast cereal, always very popular during the McDougall 10-day live-in program.

FOR THE OATS
2½ cups water
1 cup steel-cut oats
Pinch of ground cinnamon or mace (optional)

FOR THE BLUEBERRY TOPPING
1 cup blueberries
⅛ cup agave nectar

1. Place the water in a saucepan and bring to a boil. Stir in the oats and cinnamon or mace, if using. Turn off heat, cover, and let rest overnight.

2. In the morning, mix well and add a bit more water or some nondairy milk of your choice if too thick. Cover and let simmer over low heat for about 10 minutes, stirring occasionally.

3. To make the topping, place the blueberries and agave nectar in a small saucepan. Cook over low heat until blueberries soften into a syrup-like consistency, stirring occasionally.

4. Remove from heat and let rest for 5 minutes before using or let cool and refrigerate. Serve warm or chilled over the oats.

TIPS

Steel-cut oats take a long time to cook, so I always recommend that they be soaked overnight to cut the cooking time down to about 10 minutes.

The blueberry topping can also be made ahead of time and kept in the refrigerator.

LEMON-LIME GREEN SMOOTHIE

MAKES 1 SERVING

RECIPE BY TRACY RUSSELL

½ cup water
¼ lemon, peeled
¼ lime, peeled

1 small frozen banana, peeled
½ cup green grapes
1 cup curly kale, stems removed

1. Add liquid to blender, followed by soft fruit and remaining ingredients. Add the greens to your blender last.

2. Blend on high for 30–45 seconds (depending on your blender) or until the smoothie is creamy.

ORANGE-GRAPEFRUIT SMOOTHIE

MAKES 1 SERVING

RECIPE BY TRACY RUSSELL

1 orange, peeled and deseeded
½ grapefruit, peeled and deseeded

½ cup frozen pineapple, cubed
½ teaspoon pure vanilla extract

1. Add all ingredients to blender.
2. Blend on high for 30–45 seconds (depending on your blender) or until the smoothie is creamy.

CARROT-PAPAYA SMOOTHIE

MAKES 1 SERVING

RECIPE BY TRACY RUSSELL

½ cup carrot juice
1 banana, peeled

1 cup papaya, cubed
½ teaspoon ground cinnamon

1. Add all ingredients to blender.
2. Blend on high for 30–45 seconds (depending on your blender) or until the smoothie is creamy.

APPETIZERS
&
SALADS

SPICY GARBANZO SPREAD | 99

FANCIFUL & FRESH FARMERS' MARKET CEVICHE

MAKES 4 SERVINGS

RECIPE BY CHRISTINA ROSS

This bright and light ceviche features gorgeous summer vegetables that you are guaranteed to find all year round at your local grocery store and, depending on where you live, you may even be lucky enough to grab all of these summer veggies from your local farmers' market.

1 large heirloom tomato
1 large cucumber
1 small zucchini
1 avocado
1 ear corn, cut off the cob (about ½ cup), or ½ cup canned corn
5 cloves garlic, minced
1 jalapeño
1 Fresno pepper or red jalapeño (ripens red when left on vine)
3 limes, juiced

1 lemon, juiced
⅛ teaspoon crushed red pepper
¼ teaspoon sea salt
1 teaspoon mango honey
4 stems spring onion
¼ cup cilantro leaves

1. Dice the tomato, cucumber, zucchini, and avocado equally in size.

2. Cut corn from cob (no need to cook) or use ½ cup canned.

3. Set all the veggies into a shallow glass dish—a glass pie dish works great.

4. Peel and mince the garlic cloves. Deseed and mince the peppers.

5. In a small mixing bowl, add the minced garlic and peppers along with the lime juice, lemon juice, sea salt, red pepper flakes, and honey, then whisk until well mixed. Pour mixture over the veggies in your glass dish.

6. Chop the spring onions and cilantro leaves, then add them to the veggie dish. Give everything a good stir until well incorporated and serve.

7. For a fanciful presentation, garnish with lime curls. Serve on top of romaine or butter lettuce leaves, wrapped in tortillas, or just grab a spoon and dig in.

"MAGICAL" APPLESAUCE VINAIGRETTE

MAKES ABOUT ½ CUP   RECIPE BY DREENA BURTON

This dressing uses applesauce to emulsify the ingredients and produce a surprisingly thick vinaigrette that is virtually fat free!

¼ cup unsweetened applesauce
2 tablespoons apple cider vinegar
1 tablespoon balsamic vinegar
1 teaspoon mild miso (such as brown rice miso)
¾–1 teaspoon Dijon mustard

¼ teaspoon cumin
⅛ teaspoon ground cinnamon
1–1½ tablespoons maple syrup or more to taste (see Tip)
¼ teaspoon sea salt or more to taste
Freshly ground black pepper to taste

1. Using an immersion blender and deep cup (if using a blender, you may need to double the batch for enough blending volume), combine all ingredients, whizzing through until very smooth.

2. Taste, and if you'd like it a little sweeter add another teaspoon or so of maple syrup. Season to taste with additional salt and pepper as well. If you'd like a thinner dressing, simply add a couple of teaspoons of water and blend through again.

> **TIP**
>
> You may want to start with 1 tablespoon maple syrup and then adjust to add more if desired. The applesauce is also naturally sweet, so it's a personal preference how sweet you like your salad dressings.

POMEGRANATE VINAIGRETTE

MAKES 8–10 SERVINGS   RECIPE BY HEATHER CROSBY

Enjoy this scrumptious dressing on Confetti Kale Salad (p. 72) or tossed with steamed veggies, lentil sprouts, and toasted seeds for an easy, nutrient-packed meal.

¼ cup and 2 tablespoons pomegranate juice

3 tablespoons red wine vinegar

2 tablespoons vegetable stock or water

5–7 cashews

1 tablespoon maple syrup or Sucanat

2 teaspoons lime juice

Pinch of fine ground sea salt

Freshly ground black pepper

1. Place all ingredients in the blender and mix until smooth or use a whisk and some elbow grease to mix your vinaigrette.

2. Sprinkle on your favorite salad or sautéed veggies.

TIPS

If you have a juicer, prepare your own pomegranate juice using fresh arils (aka seeds).

Store in an airtight glass container in the fridge for up to two weeks.

SPICY ALMONDS

MAKES 8+ SERVINGS   RECIPE BY HEATHER CROSBY

Flavorful almonds that are delicious alone as a snack or chopped and sprinkled onto recipes like Confetti Kale Salad (p. 72).

1 cup raw almonds	1 teaspoon chili powder
1 tablespoon lime juice	¼ teaspoon fine ground sea salt
1 tablespoon Sucanat	Pinch of cayenne pepper

1. Preheat oven to 350°F and line a baking sheet with parchment paper.
2. Mix all ingredients in a bowl until almonds are thoroughly coated.
3. Spread evenly onto baking sheet in a single layer. Make sure the almonds have room for heat to reach sides.
4. Bake for no longer than 5–7 minutes. Remove from oven and slide parchment off baking sheet onto counter top so almonds can cool.

TIPS

For more lime flavor, add a pinch of lime zest to mix before toasting.

Add sesame seeds to your mixture before toasting for flavor, color, and texture.

CONFETTI KALE SALAD

MAKES 4–6 SERVINGS RECIPE BY HEATHER CROSBY

This salad is inspired by one of my favorite Chicago restaurants. It's an unexpected, party-style combination of Mexican flavors that will make a kale fan out of, well, anyone. Try it and see.

7–10 large leaves kale, stems removed
Handful of diced red onion
Handful of diced red pepper, ribs removed and
  seeded
Handful of fresh cilantro leaves
Unsulfured, unsweetened (or naturally
  sweetened) dried cranberries

Pomegranate Vinaigrette (p. 68)
1–2 tablespoons toasted sesame seeds
Spicy Almonds (p. 71)
Handful of non-GMO tortilla chips, crushed
  (optional)

1. Tear and massage kale for about 3–5 minutes until softened, dark, and in bite-size pieces. A pinch of fine ground sea salt will help speed up the softening process and add flavor and trace minerals.

2. Toss kale, onion, pepper, cilantro, cranberries, and vinaigrette together.

3. Top with sesame seeds, almonds, and tortilla chips (if desired), and serve.

TIPS

For extra color, use a medley of yellow, orange, and red peppers.

Since kale is so hardy, you can store this salad (even dressed) in the fridge for 2–3 days.

PLANT PROTEIN

What foods do you think of when you hear "protein"? "Probably not spinach and kale, although those plants have about twice as much protein, per calorie, as a lean cut of beef,"* Dr. Campbell says in *Whole*.

*Whole, p. 31

FESTIVE KALE SALAD

MAKES 2–4 SERVINGS   RECIPE BY LAURA THEODORE

This slightly sweet and crunchy combination makes a satisfying luncheon salad or festive first course for a holiday meal. The lemon tenderizes the kale, transforming it into a delightful alternative to your everyday green salad.

FOR THE DRESSING
3 tablespoons fresh lemon juice
3 tablespoons maple syrup

FOR THE SALAD
6–8 cups very thinly sliced, lightly packed
    curly kale, washed and dried
½ cup dried cranberries or dried cherries
⅓ cup chopped walnuts
Sea salt to taste (optional)
Freshly ground pepper to taste (optional)

1. Put the lemon juice and maple syrup in a small bowl and briskly whisk until smooth.
2. Put the kale, cranberries or cherries, and walnuts in a large bowl. Pour about ¾ of the dressing over the salad and toss gently until the kale, cranberries or cherries, and walnuts are evenly coated. Taste and add the remaining dressing, if desired.
3. Cover and let stand at room temperature for about 20 minutes before serving. Just before serving, top with a few grinds of sea salt and pepper, if desired.

TIPS

This salad can be made several hours in advance. If you will not be serving it within 20 minutes of preparation, cover and refrigerate it for up to 4 hours.

Pair this appealing dish with crusty bread to enhance the delicate flavors.

KALE SALAD

MAKES 4 SERVINGS

RECIPE BY LEANNE CAMPBELL

FOR THE SALAD

6 large stalks kale
½ onion, finely chopped
1 can garbanzo beans
1 large tomato, diced
1 large pepper, diced
½ cup toasted pine nuts, optional

FOR THE DRESSING

6 tablespoons seasoned rice vinegar
2 tablespoons water
1 teaspoon agave nectar
2 heaping tablespoons nutritional yeast
¼ teaspoon salt

1. Begin by ripping the kale from the stalk into small bite-size pieces. Rub the kale several times between your hands until soft and slightly wilted.

2. Add the remaining salad ingredients.

3. In a separate bowl, mix together all the dressing ingredients. Pour over the salad and serve.

LAND AND SEA SOBA SALAD

MAKES 4–6 SERVINGS  RECIPE BY CHRISTY MORGAN

This delicious summer salad was inspired by Barb Jurecki-Humphrey's cooking class at the 2009 French Meadows Macro Summer Camp.

FOR THE SALAD
1 8-ounce package soba noodles (yam or
    mugwort kinds have more protein)
1 carrot, julienned
3 leaves Napa cabbage, sliced
4 leaves kale, chopped, or 1 cup broccoli
¼ cup hiziki (or arame if not available), soaked
    in ¾ cup water
1 cup tofu, steamed or fried
2 teaspoons soy sauce or tamari
Toasted sesame seeds for garnish

FOR THE DRESSING
⅓ cup soy sauce or tamari
¼ cup brown rice vinegar
2 teaspoons fresh ginger or ginger juice
Pinch of smoked sea salt
2 tablespoons maple syrup

1. Cook soba according to directions on package.

2. Whisk dressing ingredients together.

3. Remove noodles from water, toss with dressing, and set aside.

4. Keep water boiling for blanching vegetables. Blanch veggies, except hiziki, until lightly cooked and vibrant in color. Remove with skimmer and toss veggies with noodles.

5. In a small pot, simmer hiziki with new water and soy sauce or tamari until all liquid is absorbed.

6. Steam or fry tofu in a skillet until lightly browned on both sides.

7. Toss all ingredients with noodles and veggies. Sprinkle toasted sesame seeds on top and serve immediately.

CAESAR SALAD, JAZZY-STYLE

MAKES 4–6 SERVINGS   RECIPE BY LAURA THEODORE

This vegan version of a traditional favorite adds a classic flair to any meal. Freshly prepared croutons add a real punch and tofu imparts a creamy consistency to the delightfully authentic-tasting dressing.

12 cups lightly packed romaine lettuce, washed, dried, and cut into bite-size pieces
Caesar Salad Dressing (p. 82)

FOR THE CROUTONS
5–6 slices very fresh whole-grain bread
1 teaspoon garlic powder
1 tablespoon Italian seasoning

1. Cover and refrigerate the prepared lettuce to allow it to crisp up.

2. Preheat oven to 400°F. Line a large, rimmed baking sheet with unbleached parchment paper.

3. Cut each slice of bread into nine equally sized pieces.

4. Put the bread cubes and garlic powder into a medium bowl and stir gently to evenly coat the bread cubes.

5. Add the Italian seasoning and stir to evenly coat. Spread the seasoned bread cubes in an even layer on the prepared baking sheet.

6. Bake for 12–15 minutes, turning once, until the bread cubes are golden and crisp. Put the baking sheet on a wire rack. Let the croutons cool for 5–10 minutes.

7. Place the dressing in a large bowl. Add lettuce and croutons. Toss well to thoroughly coat the lettuce and croutons with the dressing.

CAESAR SALAD DRESSING

                                          RECIPE BY LAURA THEODORE

For years I yearned for a delicious vegan version of this classic dressing, and I was really jazzed when I came up with this delightful mix of easy ingredients. The capers stand in beautifully for anchovies and the tofu replaces the egg with ease. Deeeeee-lish!

8 ounces firm regular tofu, drained
2 tablespoons fresh lemon juice
2 teaspoons capers, drained and rinsed
1 heaping teaspoon Dijon mustard

1 medium clove garlic
⅛ teaspoon sea salt
Freshly ground pepper to taste

1. Put the tofu, lemon juice, capers, Dijon, garlic, and salt in a blender and process until smooth and creamy.

2. If the mixture seems too thick, add a bit of water, 1 tablespoon at a time, to achieve the desired consistency.

3. Add freshly ground pepper to taste.

QUINOA SALAD WITH CURRANTS AND PISTACHIOS SEE PICTURE ON PAGE 2

MAKES 16 SERVINGS

RECIPE BY CHEF AJ

1 16-ounce package quinoa, cooked and
   cooled (about 8 cups)
1 cup lime juice and zest (from about 8 limes)
½ cup finely chopped scallions
1 cup finely chopped Italian parsley

1 cup finely chopped mint
2 cups currants
2 cups raw pistachios
1 cup pomegranate seeds (optional, if in
   season)

1. Prepare quinoa according to the directions on the package.
2. Place in a large bowl and allow to cool.
3. Juice and zest limes and pour over quinoa.
4. Add remaining ingredients and mix well.
5. Chill before serving.

FIESTA QUINOA SALAD

MAKES 5–7 SERVINGS   RECIPE BY CHRISTY MORGAN

This Mexican-inspired quinoa salad uses both regular and red quinoa for added texture and beauty.

FOR THE SALAD

1 cup white quinoa, washed and drained
¼ cup red quinoa, washed and drained (see Tip)
2 ears corn, cut off the cob (about 1 cup)
2 cups water
Pinch of sea salt
1½ cups cooked or 1 15-ounce can black beans, drained and rinsed
¼ cup yellow pepper, finely diced
¼ cup tomatoes, diced
¼ cup cilantro leaves

FOR THE DRESSING

2 teaspoons lime zest
2 tablespoons lime juice
2 teaspoons ground cumin
2 teaspoons chili powder
3 tablespoons tamari
1 tablespoon maple syrup
2 teaspoons apple cider vinegar

1. Place quinoa, corn, and water in a medium saucepan with pinch of salt and bring to a boil. Simmer covered for 20 minutes over low heat.

2. Meanwhile, whisk the dressing ingredients in a small bowl until well combined.

3. Fluff quinoa with a fork, place in medium bowl, and stir in the black beans, veggies, cilantro, and dressing. Season with more salt if desired.

4. Serve immediately or serve warm or cold the next day.

TIP

If you can't find red quinoa, you can use all white.

FRESH CORN SALAD

MAKES 4 SERVINGS   RECIPE BY LEANNE CAMPBELL

FOR THE SALAD

2 tablespoons vegetable stock
2½ cups corn
1 cup diced cucumber
1 cup diced green pepper
1 large tomato, diced
1 small red onion, finely diced

FOR THE DRESSING

⅓ cup seasoned rice vinegar
2 tablespoons water
¼ teaspoon salt
¼ teaspoon dried oregano

1. In a small saucepan, add vegetable stock and corn. Cook on high for 3–5 minutes.

2. In a separate bowl, combine cucumber, green pepper, tomato, onion, and cooked corn.

3. For the dressing, mix all the ingredients in a separate cup and then pour over corn salad. Either serve immediately or chill for 2–3 hours.

CARROT AND MAPLE-WALNUT SALAD

MAKES 3–4 SERVINGS RECIPE BY LAURA THEODORE

There are just five ingredients in this delightful salad, making it quick to prep but totally delicious to eat! This makes a great choice for a kid's lunchbox or any portable meal.

1¼ cups grated carrots
½ cup chopped walnuts
⅓ cup raisins

2 tablespoons maple syrup
¼ teaspoon sea salt

1. Put all of the ingredients in a medium bowl and stir gently until well combined.
2. Refrigerate for 2–4 hours. Serve chilled.

SESAME COLESLAW SALAD

MAKES 6 SERVINGS

RECIPE BY LEANNE CAMPBELL

FOR THE SALAD

4 cups grated cabbage
2 large carrots, grated
2 sour apples, diced
½ daikon, diced
1 red pepper, diced
2 stalks celery, chopped
1 cup sunflower seeds

FOR THE DRESSING

⅓ cup sesame tahini
2 large cloves garlic, crushed
⅓ cup fresh lemon juice
½ teaspoon salt
⅓ cup water

1. In a large bowl, mix all the salad ingredients.
2. In a separate bowl, mix the dressing ingredients and then pour over the salad. Serve immediately.

GREEN PAPAYA SALAD

MAKES 4 SERVINGS

RECIPE BY ANI PHYO

Green Papaya Salad is served by most street vendors in Thailand. It's a healthy salad made of shredded papaya seasoned with fresh lime juice, savory garlic, and spicy Thai red chilies.

FOR THE DRESSING

½ teaspoon garlic or to taste

¼–½ teaspoon chopped red chili pepper (from about 1 whole Thai red chili), more or less to taste

½ cup chopped green bean, cut into 1¼-inch lengths

1 tablespoon Nama Shoyu or 1 tablespoon Bragg's Liquid Aminos

2 tablespoons lime juice

2 tablespoons agave syrup

2 tablespoons chopped almonds

FOR THE SALAD

2 cups peeled and shredded green papaya

½ cup shredded carrot (about 1 small carrot)

½ cup shredded green cabbage

½ cup halved cherry tomatoes

¼ cup fresh cilantro leaves for garnish

1. Grind garlic and chilies in a food processor.

2. Add green beans and grind into small pieces.

3. Add Nama Shoyu, lime juice, agave syrup, and almonds, and pulse to mix well.

4. Place salad ingredients in a large mixing bowl. Toss with dressing.

5. Serve on four plates and garnish with cilantro leaves.

Dressing will keep for 4–5 days in fridge. Salad will keep for 2 days when stored separately. Tossed salad will keep for 1 day in fridge.

I love spice and like to use a strong chili that's full of kick. But feel free to adjust the amount of spice to a level that works for you. Since the spiciest part of the chili is in the seeds, consider removing them from your chili pepper to decrease the spice level. And if you want a mellower garlic flavor, cut down the garlic to taste.

For this recipe, choose an unripe papaya that's green and very firm, so that you'll be able to shred it.

TROPICAL THREE-BEAN SALAD

MAKES 5–7 SERVINGS RECIPE BY CHRISTY MORGAN

This salad is made with three of my favorite types of beans, which I like to cook from scratch.

½ cup dried kidney beans, soaked 5–8 hours, or 1 15-ounce can, drained and rinsed
½ cup dried white beans, soaked 5–8 hours, or 1 15-ounce can, drained and rinsed
½ cup dried garbanzo beans, soaked 5–8 hours, or 1 15-ounce can, drained and rinsed
1-inch piece kombu

1 mango, chopped
Pinch of sea salt and black pepper
1 large heirloom tomato, chopped, or 2 cups chopped Roma tomato
1 avocado, cubed
1 lime, juiced
1 teaspoon ground cumin
Dash of ground cinnamon and coriander

1. If you have a pressure cooker, cook all three beans together according to manufacturer's directions with a piece of kombu, then drain, discard kombu, and place in medium bowl.

2. Let beans cool slightly, then combine all ingredients with beans and let stand 15 minutes for flavors to meld. Add more salt to taste if desired.

TIP

The beans can all be soaked in the same bowl and cooked together in a pot or pressure cooker because they take about the same time to cook.

GARBANZO-SPINACH SALAD

MAKES 4–6 SERVINGS

RECIPE BY JOHN AND MARY MCDOUGALL

This is one of our favorite salads and very often we eat this right after putting it together. It also keeps well in the refrigerator for several days.

3 15-ounce cans garbanzo beans, drained and rinsed
2 cups loosely packed chopped fresh spinach
½ cup chopped red bell pepper

½ cup chopped yellow bell pepper
3 green onions, finely chopped
½ cup oil-free Italian dressing
Freshly ground pepper

1. Combine garbanzo beans and vegetables in a bowl.
2. Pour dressing over and toss to mix.
3. Season with freshly ground pepper.
4. Refrigerate for 1–2 hours for best flavor.

THE FIRST STEP

You're convinced by all the information you've read about the benefits of eating a whole foods, plant-based diet and you want to start immediately. But how? Dr. Campbell explains that the most important step is just to change the way you eat. The diet is simple: "Eat whole, plant-based foods, with little or no added oil, salt, or refined carbohydrates like sugar or white flour . . . There is nothing more convincing than experiencing the change for oneself."* The delicious recipes in this book help too!

*Whole, p. 289

PERFECT PESTO-STUFFED MUSHROOMS

The first time Rip Esselstyn came to my home for dinner, he ate the whole dozen of these by himself!

12 mushrooms
1 cup pine nuts
2 cloves garlic

1 tablespoon yellow miso
1 cup fresh basil
1 lemon, juiced (about ¼ cup), or to taste

1. Destem mushrooms (remove some of the caps' centers if necessary), and set aside.

2. Place the rest of the ingredients in a food processor and process until smooth.

3. Fill the mushroom cups with pesto stuffing and bake for 30 minutes at 350°F until tops are browned.

TIP

For a low-fat version, substitute 1 can cannellini beans, drained and rinsed, for the nuts.

SPICY GARBANZO SPREAD SEE PICTURE ON PAGE 63

MAKES 1½ CUPS   RECIPE BY JOHN AND MARY MCDOUGALL

This makes a delicious sandwich spread or wrap filling, a dip for raw vegetables, or a stuffing for pita bread.

1 15-ounce can garbanzo beans, drained and rinsed
2 green onions, chopped
1½ tablespoons grated ginger
1 tablespoon soy sauce

1 teaspoon rice vinegar
½ teaspoon minced fresh garlic
½ teaspoon agave nectar
Dash of Sriracha hot sauce (optional)

1. Place all ingredients (except hot sauce, if using) in a food processor and process until smooth.
2. Taste and add hot sauce as desired.
3. Refrigerate for at least 1 hour to allow flavors to blend.

ROASTED TOMATO AND GARLIC HUMMUS

MAKES 4 CUPS   RECIPE BY DREENA BURTON

Tomatoes and garlic are first roasted in an herbed marinade and then pureed with cooked garbanzo beans and tahini. This may be quite an unconventional "hummus," but it is delicious nonetheless!

1½ pounds Roma (or other) tomatoes, cut in
  half and juices gently squeezed out (see Tips)
8–9 large cloves garlic, cut in quarters or
  smaller
2 tablespoons balsamic vinegar
½ tablespoon tamari (or coconut aminos for
  soy-free option)
1 teaspoon blackstrap molasses
2 teaspoons dried oregano

2 teaspoons dried basil
⅛ teaspoon sea salt
Freshly ground black pepper to taste
2 14-ounce cans garbanzo beans, drained and
  rinsed (about 3½ cups)
¾–1 teaspoon sea salt or to taste
1–2 tablespoons tahini (I like 1 tablespoon,
  but you might like it creamier with
  2 tablespoons)

1. Preheat oven to 450°F.

2. Place tomatoes cut-side up in a glass baking dish or small rimmed baking sheet lined with parchment paper. Insert the garlic pieces into the seedy portions of the tomatoes to keep them moist while roasting.

3. In a small bowl, combine the balsamic, tamari or aminos, molasses, oregano, and basil. Drizzle mixture over tomatoes. Sprinkle the salt and pepper over top of the tomatoes.

4. Place tomatoes in oven and bake for 40–45 minutes until tomatoes are very soft and a little caramelized. Remove from oven and let cool.

5. While tomatoes are cooking, add the garbanzo beans, salt (starting with ¾ teaspoon), and tahini to a food processor. Puree to break up.

6. Add the cooled (or slightly warm) tomatoes to the food processor, scraping all the juices from the dish/parchment with a spatula. (There is a lot of flavor in those caramelized juices, so get them off and into the processor!) Process until well combined.

7. Taste, and if you'd like extra salt or pepper, add to taste and puree through.

TIPS

I like using Roma tomatoes because they are dense and meaty, with less seeds than other tomatoes. But if you have other beautifully ripe tomatoes, you can substitute.

Top your hummus with rehydrated sun-dried tomatoes, pitted olives, or sliced green onions.

Serve at room temperature with whole-grain crackers, breads, or tortilla chips. Try spreading in a wrap, using a sprouted tortilla or collard/lettuce leaves. Make a "hummus salad"—assemble a veggie-dense salad and then top with a mound of this hummus. Use as a layer on pizza, topping with veggies of choice, plus olives and capers. Try baking the mixture until heated through and serve over quinoa, rice, or other whole grains, and top with sliced avocado.

SOUPS
&
CHILIS

RED LENTIL CHILI | 119

BEST BUTTERNUT BISQUE

MAKES 6–8 SERVINGS

RECIPE BY LAURA THEODORE

Thick and creamy in texture, this bisque is a true showstopper, perfect for any cold-weather meal. Whether presented as an elegant first course, hearty luncheon entrée, or main dish supper soup, the butternut squash assures a velvety consistency and buttery taste.

6 cups cubed butternut squash (1-inch cubes)
4 cups cauliflower florets
½ cup chopped onion (from 1 small onion)
1 teaspoon Italian or all-purpose seasoning
2 apples, peeled and chopped
1 teaspoon ground cinnamon

¼ teaspoon ground ginger
¼ teaspoon sea salt
2½ cups vegetable stock, divided, plus more as needed
2 tablespoons maple syrup, divided

1. Fit a steamer basket into a large pot with a tight-fitting lid. Add 2 inches of cold water, then add the squash. Cover, bring to a boil, and steam for 7 minutes.

2. Add the cauliflower and onion. Sprinkle with the Italian or all-purpose seasoning and steam for 20 minutes more or until the squash and cauliflower are both very soft.

3. Put the squash mixture in a large bowl. Let cool for 15 minutes.

4. Add the apples, cinnamon, ginger, and salt and stir to coat.

5. Put half of the mixture in a blender. Add 1¼ cups vegetable stock and 1 tablespoon maple syrup and process until smooth. Pour into a soup pot.

6. Put the second half of the squash mixture in the blender. Add the remaining 1¼ cups vegetable stock and 1 tablespoon maple syrup, and process until smooth. Add to the soup pot, and then stir the two batches together. If the soup seems too thick, add more vegetable stock to taste.

7. Put the pot over medium-low heat, cover, and simmer, stirring often, until heated through, about 10 minutes. To serve, ladle the soup into bowls.

TIPS

This soup may be made up to 24 hours ahead of time. If making in advance, let the soup cool after blending, then pour the cooled soup into an airtight container and refrigerate.

To reheat the soup, pour it into a pot. If soup seems too thick, add more vegetable stock to taste. Cook for about 15 minutes over medium-low heat, stirring often, until heated through.

BLACK BEAN SOUP WITH SWEET POTATOES

MAKES 4–5 SERVINGS    RECIPE BY DREENA BURTON

This soup has an irresistible quality; the flavors are deep and earthy with some sweetness from the potatoes. Don't let the number of ingredients intimidate you—they build layers of flavor, but this soup is not at all difficult to make!

3 cups and 1–2 tablespoons water, divided
1½–1¾ cups chopped onion (from 1 large onion)
1½ cups chopped red and green peppers combined
1¼ teaspoons sea salt
Freshly ground black pepper to taste
2 teaspoons cumin seeds
2 teaspoons dried oregano leaves
¼ teaspoon ground allspice
¼ teaspoon crushed red pepper, more or less to taste
4 medium-large cloves garlic, minced or grated

3 14- or 15-ounce cans black beans (about 4½–5 cups), drained and rinsed, divided
2 tablespoons tomato paste
1 tablespoon balsamic vinegar
2 tablespoons fresh lime juice
½–1 teaspoon maple syrup
1 bay leaf
1½ cups diced small yellow sweet potato or white potato
Chopped cilantro for garnish
Lime wedges for garnish
Chopped avocado tossed with lemon juice and dash of salt for garnish

1. In a large pot over medium-high heat, add 1 tablespoon water, onion, red and green peppers, salt, pepper, cumin seeds, oregano, allspice, and crushed red pepper.

2. Let cook for 5–7 minutes until onion and peppers start to soften.

3. Add garlic. Cover, decrease heat to medium, and let cook another few minutes to soften garlic—if veggies are sticking or burning, add another splash of water.

4. After a few minutes of cooking, add 3½ cups beans, remaining 3 cups water, tomato paste, balsamic vinegar, lime juice, and maple syrup (starting with ½ teaspoon).

5. Using an immersion blender, puree soup until fairly smooth.

6. Increase heat to bring to boil, add bay leaf and diced sweet potatoes. Once boiling, decrease heat and let simmer for 20–30 minutes.

7. Add remaining cup of black beans and extra maple syrup, if desired.

8. Stir through, let simmer for another few minutes, then serve, topping with cilantro, if desired, and lime wedges or with some chopped seasoned avocado or a simple guacamole.

CARROT SOUP

MAKES 1 SERVING

RECIPE BY LINDSAY NIXON

This soup is an easy, light, and filling lunch when paired with a salad.

2 cups vegetable stock
4 carrots, peeled and diced
1 red apple, cored and diced

¼ cup nondairy milk, plus more as needed
Mild yellow curry powder or ground ginger

1. Line a saucepan with a thin layer of stock and sauté carrots over high heat until they start to soften, about 4 minutes.

2. Add apples, plus more stock if needed, then decrease heat to medium and cover.

3. Cook for another 1–2 minutes until apples and carrots are fork-tender (apples will take on a golden yellow coloring).

4. Transfer to a blender and blend until smooth, adding more stock as necessary—I usually add at least 1 cup. Return to pot.

5. Stir in ¼ cup nondairy milk. Add curry powder or ground ginger to taste, starting with ¼ teaspoon. If you go overboard with the spice or your apple is too sweet, add more nondairy milk.

6. Serve warm.

CREAMY BROCCOLI SOUP

MAKES 3–4 SERVINGS

RECIPE BY LAURA THEODORE

This delicate, warming soup makes a lovely light lunch or an ideal starter course for a formal soirée.

6 cups broccoli florets
1 clove garlic, chopped
2 cups nondairy milk, plus more as needed
1 teaspoon regular or reduced-sodium tamari,
  more or less to taste

1 teaspoon all-purpose seasoning
¼ teaspoon sea salt
Pinch of cayenne pepper
Freshly ground pepper to taste

1. Fit a steamer basket into a medium saucepan with a tight-fitting lid. Add 2 inches of cold water, then add the broccoli. Cover and bring to a boil. Steam the broccoli until crisp-tender, about 7 minutes.

2. Put the steamed broccoli, garlic, nondairy milk, tamari, all-purpose seasoning, salt, and cayenne pepper in a blender and process on low until smooth, making sure to leave air space at top of blender to allow steam to escape. If the soup is too thick, add more nondairy milk, 2 tablespoons at a time, to achieve the desired consistency, pulsing or blending briefly after each addition.

3. Put the soup in a medium soup pot and cook over medium-low heat until heated through, stirring often. Season with pepper. If soup is too thick, add more nondairy milk. Serve immediately in deep soup bowls with whole-grain crackers or crusty bread on the side.

CREAMY CAULIFLOWER BISQUE

MAKES 4 SERVINGS RECIPE BY LAURA THEODORE

Creamy is the operative word for this opulent offering. Steamed cauliflower harmonized with nondairy milk and other savory seasonings makes for a bisque that will prompt your diners to ask, "Is there any dairy in this soup?"

1 medium head cauliflower, cut into florets
1 cup vegetable stock, plus more as needed
¼ cup and 2 tablespoons unsweetened nondairy milk, plus more as needed

½ teaspoon ground cumin
¼ teaspoon sea salt
⅛ teaspoon freshly ground pepper (optional)

1. Fit a steamer basket into a medium saucepan with a tight fitting lid. Add 2 inches of cold water, then add the cauliflower. Cover and bring to a boil. Steam the cauliflower florets for about 20 minutes until tender.

2. Put the cauliflower, vegetable stock, nondairy milk, cumin, salt, and pepper, if using, in a blender and process until smooth.

3. Add more stock or nondairy milk, ¼ cup at a time, to achieve the desired consistency.

4. Pour into a medium saucepan, cover, and cook over medium heat for about 10 minutes, stirring often, until heated through. Serve piping hot.

TIP

After the soup is blended, it may be cooled thoroughly, packed in a tightly sealed container, and stored in the refrigerator for up to 24 hours. To serve, pour into a medium saucepan, cover, and simmer over medium-low heat for about 20 minutes, stirring often, until heated through.

EVERYTHING MINESTRONE

MAKES 8 SERVINGS   RECIPE BY LINDSAY NIXON

This is a terrific end-of-the-week recipe when you need to clean out your fridge before the next shopping trip, because you could really add anything to it. It also has that slowly-simmered-all-day taste even though it comes together quickly.

1 small onion, diced

4 garlic cloves, minced

Crushed red pepper (optional)

1 tablespoon Italian seasoning

3 cups sliced or chopped vegetables

2 cups vegetable stock

1 tablespoon red wine vinegar

1 8-ounce can tomato sauce

1 14-ounce can diced tomatoes

1 15-ounce can white beans (optional)

Salt and pepper to taste

1. Line a large pot with a thin layer of water and sauté onion, garlic, and a pinch of crushed red pepper, if using, for a minute.

2. Add Italian seasoning and continue to cook until fragrant, about 1 minute. Add all remaining ingredients, including choice vegetables (except beans), salt, and pepper, and stir to combine.

3. Bring to a boil then cover, decrease heat to low, and let simmer until vegetables are tender, about 10–20 minutes.

4. Add beans, if using, cooked rice, or pasta (see Tips), and continue to cook until thoroughly warm.

5. Add salt and pepper to taste and serve.

TIPS

Fire-roasted tomatoes are especially good here, and feel free to substitute leftover cooked pasta or rice for the optional beans—or use all three!

I typically use carrots, zucchini, and yellow squash for the vegetables, but use whatever you have on hand.

MELLOW LENTIL "SNIFFLE SOUP"

MAKES 5–6 SERVINGS

RECIPE BY DREENA BURTON

This is one of those go-to soups that is comforting, delicious with plenty of flavor—but not spicy—and sure to chase away those winter sniffles!

1–1½ tablespoons water
1½ cups diced onion
1 cup diced celery
1 cup diced carrot
3 large cloves garlic, minced
½ teaspoon sea salt
Freshly ground black pepper to taste
¾–1 teaspoon mild curry powder

1 teaspoon paprika
¼ teaspoon dried thyme
2 cups dry red lentils
3 cups vegetable stock
3½–4½ cups water
2–3 teaspoons chopped fresh rosemary
  (see Tip)
1–1½ tablespoons apple cider vinegar

1. In a large pot on medium heat, add water, onion, celery, carrot, garlic, salt, pepper, curry powder, paprika, and dried thyme and stir to combine.

2. Cover and cook for 7–8 minutes, stirring occasionally.

3. Rinse lentils. Add lentils, vegetable stock, and 3½ cups water, and stir to combine.

4. Increase heat to bring mixture to a boil. Once boiling, decrease heat to low, cover, and let simmer for 12–15 minutes.

5. Add rosemary and let simmer for another 8–10 minutes or more until lentils are completely softened.

6. Stir in vinegar, add more water as desired to thin the soup, and season to taste with additional salt and black pepper if desired.

TIP

Fresh rosemary is exquisite in this soup, but if you don't have it, you can use dried. However, add it at the beginning of the cooking process along with the other dried spices and use less—about 1 teaspoon.

PINEAPPLE-CUCUMBER GAZPACHO

MAKES 3–5 SERVINGS

RECIPE BY CHRISTY MORGAN

I used to have a soup like this in the summer at a local café. That version had too much raw onion, so I made my own with the perfect amount. Very simple to make, this is a soup you'll love all summer long.

2 English cucumbers, peeled and chopped
1½ cups seeded and chopped green bell pepper
1 green onion, chopped (optional)
2 tablespoons tamari
1 cup cilantro
1 29-ounce can pineapple with juice or 1½ cups
   fresh pineapple with 1 cup water

1 teaspoon ground cumin
2 tablespoons fresh lemon juice
2 tablespoons fresh lime juice
Sea salt and black pepper to taste
Pineapple rings for garnish (optional)

1. Blend all ingredients in a blender until no chunks remain.
2. Season to taste with sea salt and pepper.
3. Chill for at least 15 minutes before serving.
4. Decorate with pineapple rings.

RED LENTIL CHILI SEE PICTURE ON PAGE 103

MAKES ABOUT 14 CUPS

RECIPE BY CHEF AJ

12 Deglet Noor dates, pitted
8 cloves garlic, finely minced
2 14.5-ounce cans sodium-free diced tomatoes
   (fire roasted preferred)
2 large red bell peppers, chopped
1 pound red lentils
7 cups water
1 6-ounce can sodium-free tomato paste
1 large onion, chopped

4 tablespoons apple cider vinegar
1½ tablespoons parsley flakes
1½ tablespoons oregano
1½ tablespoons sodium-free chili powder
2 teaspoons smoked paprika
½ teaspoon chipotle powder or more to taste
¼ teaspoon crushed red pepper or more
   to taste

1. In a blender, blend the dates, garlic, tomatoes, and red bell pepper, until smooth and pour into an electric pressure cooker.

2. Place all remaining ingredients in the electric pressure cooker and cook on high for 10 minutes.

3. Alternatively, place all ingredients in a slow cooker and cook on low for 8 hours.

TIP

This chili is great served over a baked potato and sprinkled with
Faux Parmesan (p. 196) and chopped scallions!

SWEET POTATO CHILI WITH KALE

MAKES 12 CUPS

There is no dish that can't be improved by the addition of kale!

1 large red onion, finely chopped

2 red bell peppers, seeded and finely diced

3 cups orange juice, divided

2 pounds sweet potatoes, diced (no need to peel if organic)

2 15-ounce cans sodium-free kidney beans

2 14.5-ounce cans sodium-free fire-roasted tomatoes (I prefer Muir Glen)

1 tablespoon sodium-free chili powder

2 teaspoons smoked paprika

¼ teaspoon chipotle powder or more to taste

8 ounces Lacinato kale, finely shredded

1. In large pot, sauté onion and bell pepper in half of the orange juice for 8–10 minutes until onion is soft and translucent.

2. Add all remaining ingredients except for the kale. Bring to a boil and then decrease heat to let simmer for 25–30 minutes until the sweet potatoes are soft but not mushy.

3. Turn off heat and stir in kale so it wilts, then serve.

4. To make in an electric pressure cooker, place all ingredients except for the kale in the cooker and cook on high pressure for 8 minutes. Stir kale in before serving.

> ### TIP
>
> This dish is great with a piece of corn bread on top!

SWEET POTATO AND YELLOW SPLIT PEA SOUP

MAKES ABOUT 16 CUPS

RECIPE BY CHEF AJ

1 pound yellow split peas
1 large onion, chopped
1 pound carrots, sliced
1 celery heart, sliced
2 large sweet potatoes, cubed
8 cups boiling water
6–8 cloves garlic, pressed
4 teaspoons dried parsley

1–2 tablespoons sodium-free seasoning
1 teaspoon dried basil
1 teaspoon dried rosemary
1 teaspoon dried oregano
1 teaspoon celery seed
1 teaspoon smoked paprika
1 bay leaf

1. Place all ingredients in an electric pressure cooker and cook on high for 8 minutes. Let pressure release naturally or release and enjoy immediately.

2. Alternatively, place all ingredients in a slow cooker and cook on low for 6–8 hours. Tastes even better the next day!

BURGERS, SANDWICHES & TACOS

QUICK BURGERS

MAKES 4 BURGERS

RECIPE BY LINDSAY NIXON

I developed these burgers in a hotel room, so they're quick, easy, and require very few ingredients. (In fact, except for the beans and a seasoning packet, I sourced all the ingredients from the complimentary "breakfast bar.") I make these burgers any time I need a super-fast meal or I'm really low on ingredients.

1 15-ounce can black beans, drained and rinsed
2 tablespoons ketchup
1 tablespoon yellow mustard

1 teaspoon granulated onion powder
1 teaspoon granulated garlic powder
⅓ cup instant oats

1. Preheat oven to 400°F.
2. Line a cookie sheet with parchment paper and set aside.
3. In a mixing bowl, mash black beans with a fork until mostly pureed but with some half beans and bean parts left.
4. Stir in condiments and spices until well combined, then mix in oats.
5. Divide into 4 equal portions and shape into thin patties.
6. Bake for 10 minutes, carefully flip over, and bake for another 5 minutes or until crusty on the outside.
7. Slap onto a bun with extra condiments and eat!

SNEAKY CHICKPEA BURGERS

MAKES 7–8 PATTIES    RECIPE BY DREENA BURTON

For those of you that need to sneak veggies into your kids at every opportunity, here's an easy way to get some in! Our girls have NO idea that these burgers have both carrots and red pepper . . . and I'll keep it that way for a while.

1 cup disc-cut carrots
½ cup chopped red bell pepper
1 medium-large clove garlic
2 14-ounce cans garbanzo beans (chickpeas), drained and rinsed
½ cup nutritional yeast
1 tablespoon tomato paste or ketchup
1 tablespoon tahini (optional)

1 teaspoon sea salt
1 teaspoon red wine vinegar
½ teaspoon Dijon mustard
Freshly ground black pepper (optional)
1 teaspoon fresh rosemary leaves or ¼ cup fresh basil leaves
1 cup rolled oats

1. In a food processor, process carrots with bell pepper and garlic until crumbly and broken down.

2. Add remaining ingredients except rolled oats and process through. Stop processor a few times and scrape down, then continue to process until smooth.

3. Add rolled oats and pulse through.

4. Remove bowl and place in fridge to chill mixture for about 30 minutes. Be sure to chill; it really makes the burgers easier to shape.

5. After chilling, take out scoops of mixture and form burgers in your hands.

6. To cook, place patties on a nonstick skillet (that has been wiped with a touch of oil) over medium or medium-high heat.

7. Let cook on one side for 7–8 minutes or until golden brown.

8. Flip and let cook for another 5–7 minutes on the other side.

9. Serve on buns with fixings of choice!

TIP

Alternatively, these patties can be baked at 400°F for about 20 minutes, flipping halfway through, though I prefer the sear and texture that pan-cooking offers.

BARBECUE PORTOBELLO SANDWICHES

MAKES 6 SERVINGS   RECIPE BY JOHN AND MARY MCDOUGALL

These sandwiches remind some people of pulled pork, but since we have never eaten a pulled pork sandwich you couldn't prove it to us. They are still great though, no matter what you call them.

1 cup fat-free barbecue sauce
1 chipotle chili in adobo sauce, minced
1 onion, chopped

3 large portobello mushrooms, stems and gills removed, chopped
6 whole-wheat buns

1. Place the barbecue sauce in a bowl. Add the minced chipotle and mix well. Set aside.

2. Place the onions and mushrooms in a large nonstick sauté pan. Cook over medium-high heat for about 10 minutes, stirring almost constantly with a spatula to keep the vegetables from sticking to the pan. The onions and mushrooms will take on a golden brown color.

3. Pour the barbecue sauce over the onions and mushrooms and mix well. Decrease heat to low and cook gently, stirring occasionally, for 10 minutes.

4. Split the buns and warm them, then ladle the barbecue mixture over the buns.

5. Top with your choice of garnishes. Serve open face or close up the buns and eat the sandwiches with your hands.

> **TIP**
>
> Try topping with coleslaw, tomatoes, sliced onions, and lettuce. (Shredded cabbage tossed with rice vinegar and lime juice makes a delicious stand-in for coleslaw.) Or try topping with sauerkraut and mustard.

PORTOBELLO WRAPS WITH SPICY ASIAN SLAW

MAKES 4 SERVINGS

RECIPE BY DEL SROUFE

This is one of my favorite lunches. Sometimes I grill the mushrooms whole and make a burger out of it, but usually I eat it like this.

½ cup rice wine vinegar
¼ cup brown rice syrup
1 tablespoon low-sodium soy sauce
4 cups coleslaw mix
½ red bell pepper, diced small
1 large jalapeño pepper, minced
½ cup chopped green onions

½ cup chopped fresh cilantro
4 medium portobello mushrooms, sliced
    ½-inch thick
1 medium yellow onion, cut into ½-inch slivers
Sea salt and black pepper to taste
4 10- or 12-inch whole-grain tortillas

1. Combine the vinegar, rice syrup, and soy sauce in a medium bowl.
2. Add the coleslaw mix, red bell pepper, jalapeño pepper, green onions, and cilantro, and mix well. Let sit for 30 minutes before serving.
3. Heat a large skillet over medium-high heat. Add the mushrooms and yellow onion, and cook, stirring frequently, for 7–8 minutes, until the vegetables are tender. Season with salt and pepper and set aside.
4. To make the wraps, lay each tortilla flat on a surface and divide the mushrooms between them. Spoon some of the slaw over the mushrooms and roll each tortilla up.

TIP

If your tortilla does not roll without cracking, warm it in a dry skillet over medium heat for a few minutes to soften it.

ADZUKI BEAN TACOS SEE PICTURE ON PAGE 123

MAKES 4 SERVINGS    RECIPE BY DEL SROUFE

Adzuki beans taste a little like black-eyed peas. Their sweetness makes them a versatile bean that you can use in any number of dishes. They are one of my favorite beans, and this recipe is one of the ways I like to eat them most. The tangy slaw provides great contrast to the sweetness of the beans.

1 medium onion, minced
1 jalapeño pepper, minced
2 cloves garlic, minced
1 large tomato, diced
2 teaspoons cumin seeds, toasted and ground
2 teaspoons ancho chili powder

Sea salt to taste
Cayenne pepper to taste
2 cups cooked adzuki beans
8 6-inch corn tortillas or taco shells
4 cups Cilantro-Lime Slaw (p. 220)

1. Sauté the onion over medium heat for 6–7 minutes.

2. Add the jalapeño pepper, garlic, tomato, cumin, chili powder, salt, and cayenne pepper.

3. Let cook for 10 minutes, then add the beans and cook for another 5 minutes or so, until heated through.

4. To serve, spoon some of the bean mixture down the center of a tortilla and top with some of the slaw.

5. Repeat with remaining tortillas.

TACO SEASONING

MAKES ABOUT ⅓ CUP (ENOUGH TO SEASON 12+ TACOS) RECIPE BY HEATHER CROSBY

Keep a batch (or five) of this seasoning on hand for quick and easy meals like tacos. Skip the store-bought packets full of preservatives and anti-caking agents and season sautéed vegetables, cooked legumes, grains, and more with this flavorful combination of spices.

Dry zest from 1 lime (optional)
2 tablespoons chili powder
1 tablespoon ground cumin
2 teaspoons fine ground sea salt

2 teaspoons ground coriander
1 teaspoon paprika
½ teaspoon freshly ground pepper
⅛ teaspoon cayenne pepper (optional)

1. This is an optional but tasty step, so I recommend it—zest 1 lime. Place the zest either in a small dish on a sunny windowsill, dry in a dehydrator, or an oven heated to 175°F for about 10–15 minutes until all moisture is gone.
2. Toss all ingredients in a bowl until well mixed.
3. Store in a cool, dark place in an airtight glass container.

TIP

If adding zest, make sure it is 100 percent dry. Water attracts mold and mold will ruin your spice mix.

BLUE CORN CHICKPEA TACOS

MAKES 8 TACOS    RECIPE BY LINDSAY NIXON

Everyone loves these tacos. I've managed to get my parents, my best friend, and just about everyone I know hooked on them. They're also one of the most popular recipes on my website, Happyherbivore.com.

1 tablespoon soy sauce
1–2 teaspoons fresh lemon or lime juice
1 tablespoon chili powder
1½ teaspoons ground cumin
1 teaspoon fine salt
1 teaspoon pepper
½ teaspoon paprika
¼ teaspoon granulated garlic powder

¼ teaspoon granulated onion powder
⅛ teaspoon cayenne powder
¼ teaspoon dried marjoram or oregano
1 15-ounce can garbanzo beans (chickpeas),
    drained and rinsed
Oil-free blue corn taco shells (see Tips)
Arugula or lettuce
1 salad tomato, diced

1. Preheat oven to 400°F.

2. Line a cookie sheet with parchment paper and set aside.

3. Whisk soy sauce, juice, and spices together, then combine with chickpeas in a bowl, stirring to combine.

4. Transfer to cookie sheet in a single layer.

5. Bake for 20–40 minutes until chickpeas are as crisp as desired.

6. Spoon chickpeas into taco shells and top with greens and tomatoes.

TIPS

To make your own baked taco shells, preheat oven to 375°F. Wrap tortillas in a damp paper towel and heat in microwave for 30 seconds. Drape each tortilla over two bars of your oven rack and bake until crispy, about 7–10 minutes.

Try serving with arugula, fresh tomatoes, and a tiny dollop of vegan sour cream on top.

LENTIL, KALE, AND QUINOA TACOS

MAKES 12+ TACOS    RECIPE BY HEATHER CROSBY

This is an updated version of one of the most popular YumUniverse.com recipes. I've received countless comments over the years, especially from the herbivore mamas out there, claiming that when they make these tacos for the family, kiddos and husbands happily mumble with mouths full of seconds, ". . . if all vegan food tastes this good, I'll never eat meat again!"

Blue corn taco shells

FOR THE FILLING
1 cup dry quinoa
½ cup dry lentils
⅓ cup Taco Seasoning (p. 133)
2–3 large leaves kale, stems removed and
  chopped

FOR THE TOPPINGS
Fresh cilantro leaves
1–2 avocados, pitted, peeled, and sliced
Fresh lime wedges

1. Soak quinoa and lentils in two separate bowls of water overnight (8–12 hours).

2. Rinse quinoa well and place in a pot. Fill pot with enough water to cover quinoa by about 1 inch. Bring to a boil uncovered, then reduce heat to medium. Cover pot and cook for 10–15 minutes until all water is absorbed. Remove from heat but leave lid on pot for 5 minutes. Fluff with fork.

3. Repeat step two using soaked lentils.

4. While the filling cooks, wash cilantro well and remove leaves. Slice avocado in half lengthwise, remove pit, remove fruit from rind, and slice into pieces. Slice lime into wedges.

5. While cooked quinoa and lentils are still warm, fold in taco seasoning and chopped kale leaves. Stir well until heat wilts the leaves. Warm over low-medium heat if necessary.

6. Toast taco shells according to manufacturer's instructions.

7. Load shells with avocado, filling, cilantro, and a squeeze of lime, and serve warm.

Wrap up this taco filling into steamed collard greens or gluten-free tortillas to make burritos.

To make a tasty taco salad, just toss recipe with loads of greens and a squeeze of lime.

Some health food stores now carry sprouted quinoa and lentils—skip the overnight soaking if you can find them.

Boil quinoa and lentils with chopped kombu and/or add dulse granules to the filling for extra trace minerals without detectable sea flavor.

ENTRÉES

HURRY CURRY QUINOA | 178

ALOO GOBI

MAKES 2 SERVINGS  RECIPE BY LINDSAY NIXON

Aloo gobi is a popular Indian dish made of potatoes (*aloo*) and cauliflower (*gobi*).

1 cup vegetable stock, divided
1 tablespoon fresh ginger, minced
2–3 cloves garlic, minced
1 small onion, diced
1 8-ounce can tomato sauce
1 teaspoon ground coriander
½ teaspoon ground cumin
Ground turmeric to taste

Paprika to taste
1 tablespoon ketchup
1 russet potato, diced
1 head cauliflower, chopped into florets
1 teaspoon garam masala, plus more as needed
Cayenne pepper to taste
Chopped fresh cilantro for garnish

1. Line a medium pot with a thin layer of vegetable stock and sauté ginger, garlic, and onion over high heat until onions are translucent.

2. Add tomato sauce, then stir in coriander, cumin, a few dashes of turmeric for color, and 1–2 dashes of paprika and ketchup.

3. Add potato and cauliflower and stir to coat everything well. Add remaining stock and stir again.

4. Cover and bring to a boil. Once boiling, decrease heat to low and let simmer for 20 minutes or until vegetables are fork-tender and soft.

5. Add 1 teaspoon garam masala and cayenne as desired. Taste, adding salt or more garam masala as needed.

6. Serve over cooked brown rice, if desired, and garnish generously with chopped fresh cilantro.

BLACK-EYED PEA BBQ STEW

MAKES 4–6 SERVINGS   RECIPE BY CHRISTY MORGAN

This hearty and filling stew will leave you feeling warm and comforted. The black-eyed peas and root vegetables are full of fiber, so it's a great meal to fill you up without much fat or calories.

1 cup dried black-eyed peas, washed
1 cup diced small rutabaga
2 stalks celery, diced
1 carrot, diced
Pinch of sea salt, plus more to taste

½ cup water
½ cup barbecue sauce
1 cup frozen peas
Black pepper to taste

1. Combine beans and water in a pressure cooker or pot, then cover. Heat over medium-high heat. Skim off any foam that forms when beans begin to boil. This is a trick to reduce gas and bloating. If using a pressure cooker, wet the gasket of the lid and lock it in place. Follow the manufacturer's instructions regarding cooking times for different beans.

2. Meanwhile, in a skillet with lid, simmer veggies with a pinch of salt and ½ cup water until tender.

3. When beans are done, drain and return to pressure cooker or pot. Add veggie mixture to beans with barbecue sauce and let simmer, covered, for 5 minutes. Add water as necessary if it starts to stick and stir occasionally.

4. Stir in peas and season with salt and pepper as needed.

TIP

To shave off 20 minutes from this recipe, use 2 15-ounce cans black-eyed peas, drained and rinsed, and skip the cooking beans step.

OVEN-BAKED CHICKPEA RATATOUILLE

MAKES 5–6 SERVINGS  RECIPE BY DREENA BURTON

This dish is much like ratatouille in appearance but uses chickpeas and an original spice combination. The flavors are complex and the preparation minimal!

3½–4 cups cooked or 2 14- or 15-ounce cans garbanzo beans (chickpeas), drained and rinsed
1¼ cups red onion, finely chopped
3–4 medium-large cloves garlic, minced
1 28-ounce can diced tomatoes (see Tips)
½ cup diced red or orange bell pepper
2 tablespoons apple cider vinegar
1 tablespoon freshly grated ginger

2 teaspoons maple syrup or agave nectar
2 teaspoons mustard seeds
2 teaspoons dried basil
1 teaspoon dried oregano
½ teaspoon dried rosemary
1 teaspoon sea salt
⅛ teaspoon ground allspice
Freshly ground black pepper to taste
2 dried bay leaves

1. Preheat oven to 400°F.
2. In a large, deep casserole dish, combine all ingredients except bay leaves.
3. Stir through until well combined, then embed bay leaves in the mixture.
4. Cover and bake for 30 minutes.
5. Stir through, cover, and bake for another 35–45 minutes until onions are tender and translucent (stir through once more during baking).
6. Remove bay leaves and serve over quinoa or brown rice.

TIPS

Use regular diced tomatoes or Italian flavored or fire-roasted for a twist.

Try making burritos with leftovers. Spoon the mixture onto whole-grain tortillas, roll up, and place in a baking dish, then bake until golden.

This makes a large batch, but portions can be refrigerated or frozen.

APPLE LENTIL DAL

MAKES 5–6 SERVINGS

RECIPE BY DREENA BURTON

The preparation for this dal-like dish is simple and unfussy. But the flavor is more complex. Just a few subtle herbs and spices combined with sweet apples and earthy red lentils make this puree simply delectable.

3½ cups and 1 tablespoon water, divided
2 cups chopped onion
½ teaspoon ground cinnamon
½–1 teaspoon cumin seeds
½ teaspoon dry mustard
1 teaspoon dried oregano leaves
½ teaspoon turmeric

1–1¼ teaspoons sea salt
2 cups red lentils, rinsed
1 cup chopped apple (peeling optional, see Tips)
2 tablespoons fresh lemon juice
Crushed red pepper or hot sauce (optional)

1. In a pot over medium-high heat, add 1 tablespoon water, onion, spices, and salt.

2. Stir through, and cover, cooking for 4–5 minutes. Keep an eye on it; add another splash of water if spices and onion are sticking.

3. Remove cover and add lentils and water.

4. Turn heat up to high, and bring mixture to a boil. Once at a boil, decrease heat to low and cover, cooking for about 15 minutes.

5. After 12–15 minutes, add the apple and lemon juice, stir through, and cook for another 5–7 minutes until the apple has softened a little but isn't entirely mushy.

6. Taste, season with additional salt or lemon juice and crushed red pepper or hot sauce, if desired, and serve.

TIPS

An apple that is not entirely sweet is preferable. It doesn't have to be a very tart variety like a Granny Smith, but perhaps a Braeburn or Honey Crisp, rather than a Golden or Red Delicious.

This is a thick puree that is wonderful served over brown short-grain or basmati rice, quinoa, or millet. When cooled, try spreading onto tortillas or collard leaves for wraps.

THAT OLD FOLK WISDOM

You've heard that "an apple a day keeps the doctor away," but have you ever wondered why? What is it about the apple that promotes health? According to *Whole*, "[T]here is a treasure trove of vitamin C–like compounds in apples. These include other antioxidants with names like quercetin, catechin, phlorizin, and chlorogenic acid found only in plants, each of which may exist in many forms within the apple. The list of these chemicals in apples and other fruits is long, and likely reflects just the tip of the iceberg. It's as if the inside of the apple is bigger than it looks from the outside. . . . [A]n apple does a lot more inside our bodies than all the known apple nutrients ingested in pill form. The whole apple is far more than the sum of its parts."*

*Whole, p. 153–154

LENTIL LOAF

MAKES 8 SERVINGS

RECIPE BY LINDSAY NIXON

Nothing says American like Mom's meatloaf! This Lentil Loaf hits the spot anytime I'm in the mood for a comforting down-home-cooking kind of meal.

1 cup dried lentils
2 cups vegetable stock
1 small onion
1 carrot, skinned
2 stalks celery
¼ cup ketchup

2 tablespoons yellow mustard
2 tablespoons low-sodium soy sauce
2 tablespoons nutritional yeast
1 tablespoon Italian seasoning
1 cup instant oats (see Tips)

1. Combine lentils with vegetable stock in a pot, cover, and bring to a boil.

2. Once boiling, decrease heat to low and let simmer for 20 minutes or until lentils are cooked (soft, but not mushy) and the liquid has evaporated.

3. Meanwhile, place onion, carrot, and celery in a food processor or blender and pulse until they are finely chopped—the smaller the better, but don't pulverize.

4. Transfer to a large mixing bowl and mix with ketchup, mustard, soy sauce, nutritional yeast, and Italian seasoning and set aside.

5. Preheat oven to 350°F and line a standard bread pan with parchment paper, allowing the paper to rise 2 inches above the top of the pan.

6. Once lentils are cooked, transfer to blender or food processor and pulse a few times so most of the lentils are chewed up but some half lentils remain and it's not total mush.

7. Transfer chopped lentils to the mixing bowl, add oats, and stir to combine.

8. Pour mixture into bread pan, pressing it into every corner and packing it down firmly with a spatula.

9. Bake for 40–50 minutes uncovered or until firm with a crisp outer coating.

10. Let cool in the pan for 10 minutes before serving. Place a plate on top of the pan and flip over, so the loaf flips onto the plate.

If you have rolled oats, you can pulse them a few times in your blender or food processor to make them smaller—do this first while the container is still dry.

Serve with steamed mixed vegetables and mashed potatoes.

LENTIL MARINARA SAUCE

MAKES 5 CUPS

RECIPE BY LINDSAY NIXON

This hearty marinara is very filling and scratches that pasta itch.

2 cups vegetable stock, divided
3–4 cloves garlic, minced
1 small onion, diced
2–3 tablespoons tomato paste
2 tomatoes, diced (optional)
1 15-ounce can diced tomatoes

1 tablespoon Italian seasoning
1 tablespoon red wine vinegar
½ cup red lentils
1 small jalapeño, chopped, stem discarded
Ketchup (optional)

1. Line a medium pot with a thin layer of stock and sauté garlic and onion over high heat until onion is translucent, about 2 minutes.

2. Add required remaining ingredients (starting with 2 tablespoons tomato paste) and bring to a boil.

3. Once boiling, decrease heat to low, and let simmer until lentils are soft and cooked, about 20–30 minutes.

4. Allow to cool so it's not lava hot and taste, adding more tomato paste if desired, plus salt and pepper.

5. If it's too acidic, you can add a quick squeeze of ketchup. If it's not saucy enough for you, add more stock or tomato sauce to thin it out.

TIPS

If desired, you can transfer part (or all) of the sauce to a blender and blend until smooth (I like it chunky). Fire-roasted tomatoes—instead of plain diced—also add a little something extra to this dish.

I like to serve this over spaghetti squash for a lower calorie "spaghetti" experience, but it's great on baked potatoes, broccoli, or anything you'd usually smother with marinara sauce.

The flavor intensifies over time, so make ahead if you can and look forward to leftovers!

DAD'S MARINARA

MAKES 4–6 SERVINGS   RECIPE BY LAURA THEODORE

My dad makes a fabulous marinara that is always a top request at any family gathering.

1 28-ounce can crushed tomatoes (see Tips)
1 cup water, plus more as needed
3 cloves garlic, minced, or ½ teaspoon garlic powder
1½ teaspoons dried basil

1 teaspoon dried oregano
½ teaspoon dried parsley
¼ teaspoon crushed red pepper (see Tips)
2 tablespoons good red wine (optional)
Sea salt or Himalayan pink salt to taste

1. Put the tomatoes, water, garlic, basil, oregano, parsley, and crushed red pepper in a large saucepan. If mixture seems too thick, add ¼ cup water.

2. Stir to combine. Bring to a simmer over medium heat.

3. Decrease the heat to medium-low, cover, and let simmer, stirring occasionally, for 45 minutes.

4. If desired, add the optional red wine at this point.

5. Let simmer for 15–30 minutes more or for up to 2 hours (the longer you cook it, the more developed the flavors will be).

6. Add salt to taste, if desired. Serve over whole-grain pasta of your choice.

TIPS

I use crushed tomatoes, but Dad uses canned tomato sauce.

Use ⅛ teaspoon crushed red pepper for a less spicy sauce.

The longer you cook it, the more complex the sauce becomes. Use it to top plain spaghetti or any other kind of pasta, or use it as a base for lasagna, stuffed shells, or casseroles.

SPAGHETTI AND WHEATBALLS

MAKES 3–4 SERVINGS (12–14 WHEATBALLS)   RECIPE BY LAURA THEODORE

This dish has an authentic taste and texture, making it a foolproof crowd-pleaser for any family meal. Easy enough to make for a special weeknight meal, but fancy enough to serve when hosting a casual dinner party, this dish will become a staple in your house.

1⅓ cups lightly packed, fresh, soft whole-grain
    bread crumbs (see Tips)
1 teaspoon Italian seasoning
½ teaspoon garlic powder
⅛ teaspoon sea salt
½ cup chopped walnuts

2 cups chopped mushrooms
½ cup diced onion
¾ pound spaghetti (see Tips)
3 cups jarred, low-fat, oil-free marinara sauce
    or Dad's Marinara (p. 152)

1. Preheat oven to 350°F.

2. Line a medium baking pan with unbleached parchment paper.

3. Put the bread crumbs, Italian seasoning, garlic powder, and salt in a large bowl.

4. Put the walnuts in a blender and pulse to process into coarse crumbs.

5. Add the walnuts to the bread crumbs and stir gently to incorporate.

6. Put the mushrooms and onion in a blender and process to a chunky puree.

7. Add the mushroom mixture to the walnut/bread crumb mixture and stir to incorporate.

8. Spoon out about 1½ tablespoons of the mushroom mixture and roll it into a ball. Continue in this way with the remaining mushroom mixture.

9. Arrange the rolled wheatballs on the lined baking pan.

10. Bake for 25–30 minutes. Gently rotate each wheatball and bake for 12–16 minutes more or until they are crisp and golden.

11. Bring a large pot of salted water to a boil. Add the spaghetti and cook, stirring occasionally, until tender but firm. Drain the spaghetti well.

12. Meanwhile, pour the marinara sauce into a medium saucepan. Bring the sauce to a simmer over medium-low heat.

13. Gently add the wheatballs to the sauce, 1 at a time, cover, and let simmer for 7–10 minutes.

14. To serve, put one-quarter of the spaghetti into each of four pasta bowls and top with 3–4 wheatballs. Ladle marinara sauce over the top and serve immediately.

TIPS

To make fresh bread crumbs, put 3–4 slices of whole-grain bread in a blender and process into coarse crumbs.

The wheatballs make a sensational base for a hero-style sandwich too!

CREAMY BROCCOLI & RED PEPPER MACARONI

MAKES 4–6 SERVINGS

RECIPE BY HEATHER CROSBY

This is one of the recipes that I love to try out on the biggest skeptics because they all end up loving it—always proclaiming their disbelief that it is nondairy while asking for more.

FOR THE SAUCE
1 cup cashews
1 tablespoon fresh lemon juice
¾ cup water
1 tablespoon nutritional yeast
1 clove garlic
¾ teaspoon pink Himalayan or Celtic sea salt

2 cups gluten-free macaroni noodles
1–3 tablespoons water or vegetable stock, divided
1 red pepper, ribs removed, seeded, and diced
1 cup broccoli florets
Pinch of smoked sea salt
Freshly ground pepper to taste

1. Soak cashews in a bowl of water for 4–6 hours. Rinse well.

2. Bring large pot of water to a boil. Add noodles and cook according to manufacturer's instructions.

3. Blend together all sauce ingredients until smooth and set aside.

4. While noodles cook, place 1 tablespoon water or vegetable stock in a skillet heated to medium and add diced pepper. Stir often for 7 minutes.

5. Add broccoli and remaining water or vegetable stock to skillet, stir, cover, and steam for 3–5 minutes. Remove from heat.

6. Rinse cooked noodles. Then in a large pot, mix together noodles, veggies, and sauce over medium heat. Season with more salt to taste, if necessary, and freshly ground pepper. Enjoy warm.

TIPS

You can skip the soaking step for cashews, but know that soaking helps digestion and assimilation of nutrients and adds a creamy texture to the sauce.

You can use ½ cup cashews and ½ cup sunflower seeds for the sauce or 1 cup sunflower seeds instead of cashews if you have an allergy.

CREAMY FETTUCCINE

MAKES ABOUT 2½–3 CUPS SAUCE   RECIPE BY DREENA BURTON

This sauce takes just minutes to pull together. Everything goes into a blender and then you are ready to toss a creamy, rich sauce into tender whole-grain noodles for a most satisfying, comforting meal.

¾–1 pound whole-grain pasta
½ cup soaked cashews
½ cup soaked almonds
1 tablespoon toasted pine nuts
½ tablespoon mild miso (chickpea or brown rice)
2–3 cloves garlic (less if needed for the kiddos)
½ teaspoon onion powder
1½ tablespoons fresh lemon juice

1 teaspoon sea salt
½ teaspoon Dijon mustard
½ cup nondairy milk, plus more as needed
1 cup water
1 teaspoon lemon zest
Few pinches of freshly grated nutmeg and/or freshly ground black pepper to taste
2–3 tablespoons toasted pine nuts, crushed (optional)

1. Prepare pasta according to package directions.
2. Meanwhile, in a blender, puree the cashews, almonds, pine nuts, miso, garlic, onion powder, lemon juice, salt, Dijon, milk, and water until very, very smooth.
3. Once pasta is cooked, drain it (do not rinse) and return it to the cooking pot.
4. Add the sauce (get every bit possible out of the blender!) and bring heat up to medium-low.
5. Let the sauce mixture thicken; it will take just a few minutes. If sauce is too thick, add 1–2 tablespoons milk or more to thin, and stir through over low heat.
6. Stir in lemon zest and nutmeg and/or pepper to taste.
7. Sprinkle on a few toasted pine nuts, if using, and serve with a side salad.

VARIATION

GREENS OPTION

Greens like spinach taste awfully good wilted into this pasta! Simply toss through several handfuls of baby spinach just before serving. The heat of the pasta and sauce will wilt the greens within a minute or so, just enough without overcooking.

If you'd like to use a hardier green like chopped kale, add it to the cooking water *just* before draining. Just add, submerge, then drain straight away. That will be enough time to blanch these sturdier greens, since they will continue to cook with the heat of the pasta and sauce. Proceed with the recipe and serve immediately so the greens are wilted but not overcooked.

DAIKON MUSHROOM FETTUCCINE

MAKES 2 SERVINGS

RECIPE BY CHRISTINA ROSS

This fettuccine is the perfect recipe to make when you're looking for a fresh, simple, yet sophisticated dish to serve at your next dinner party or date night. It's bursting with a creamy rich buttery flavor, yet leaves you feeling satisfied and light.

1 tablespoon and 1 teaspoon sea salt, divided
1 large daikon
1 tablespoon coconut water
1½ tablespoons minced garlic
2 tablespoons minced yellow onion

2–3 tablespoons coconut milk
½ pint sliced mushrooms
4 leaves basil, julienned
1 teaspoon hemp seeds
Black pepper to taste

1. Boil a medium pot of water and pour into heat-safe bowl. Stir in 1 tablespoon sea salt and set aside.

2. While the water is boiling, use a vegetable peeler and, starting from the top of the daikon, slice strips using little pressure to ensure a thin peel.

3. Add the daikon to the bowl of hot water and let sit for 15 minutes.

4. While the daikon "noodles" are tenderizing, make the sauce by placing the coconut water in a small pan on medium-high heat. Once pan is warmed up, add the garlic, onion, 2 tablespoons milk, and mushrooms. Stir, then cover with a lid and decrease the heat to a low simmer. Cook for 3 minutes. Sauce will bubble up and thicken; if you feel you need to add more milk, add 1 tablespoon more, stir, and cover.

5. Once mushrooms are cooked and release their juice, give them another stir and add the daikon noodles to the pan. Using tongs, mix the sauce with the noodles and plate the pasta.

6. Garnish with basil, hemp seeds, and black pepper. Serve with a side salad.

SAVORY MUSHROOM STROGANOFF

MAKES 4 SERVINGS RECIPE BY LAURA THEODORE

Thanks to meaty-tasting portobello mushrooms, this satisfying stroganoff has the rich flavor of the traditional version without all of the extra fat and calories.

1 medium sweet onion, chopped

3–4 cups vegetable stock, divided, plus more as needed

8 ounces portobello mushrooms, thinly sliced

1 teaspoon dried basil

1 teaspoon reduced-sodium tamari

Pinch of cayenne pepper

8 ounces cremini or white button mushrooms, sliced

1 tablespoon whole-wheat flour, plus more as needed (see Tip)

½ cup water, plus more as needed

Sea salt to taste

Freshly ground pepper to taste

8 ounces whole-grain rotini, fusilli, or other pasta of your choice, cooked and drained

½ cup chopped fresh flat-leaf parsley for garnish

1. Put the onion and 2 tablespoons vegetable stock in a large skillet.
2. Cook over medium-low heat, stirring occasionally, until slightly softened, about 5 minutes. Add more stock, 1 tablespoon at a time, if the onion becomes dry.
3. Add the portobello mushrooms, basil, tamari, and cayenne pepper, and cook, stirring occasionally, about 5 minutes, adding more stock 1 tablespoon at a time as needed to prevent sticking.
4. Add the cremini mushrooms and cook, stirring occasionally, until browned, about 8 minutes.
5. Stir in 1½ cups stock. Cover and let simmer, stirring occasionally, for 15–20 minutes, adding more stock as needed.
6. Put the flour and ½ cup water in a blender and process until smooth.
7. Briskly whisk the flour-water mixture into the mushrooms.
8. Cook, stirring constantly, until the liquid has thickened to form a gravy.
9. Season with salt and pepper. Serve immediately over pasta and garnish with parsley.

TIP

If the gravy is too thick, thin with additional stock to achieve the desired consistency. If the gravy is too thin, thicken with additional flour to achieve the desired consistency.

VEGETARIAN PHO WITH VEGETABLES

MAKES 4 SERVINGS

RECIPE BY ANI PHYO

Many Vietnamese people eat phở for breakfast rather than as an evening meal.

FOR THE MARINADE
¼ cup diced yellow onion
½ cup sliced button mushrooms
¼ cup Nama Shoyu or Bragg's Liquid Aminos

FOR THE STOCK
1 tablespoon grated ginger
1 teaspoon minced garlic
1 bay leaf
4 cups water, divided
4 cups kelp noodles (about 1 pound)
½ cup shredded Napa cabbage
½ cup tender greens (e.g., mustard, Bibb, red
    leaf, mache, or spinach)
⅓ cup fresh basil leaves
⅓ cup coarsely chopped fresh cilantro
2 tablespoons thinly sliced scallions

FOR THE GARNISH
1 cup bean sprouts
1 lime, cut into wedges
1 fresh red or green chili pepper, sliced
Hoisin sauce

1. Marinate onion and mushrooms by tossing in a bowl with Nama Shoyu or Bragg's Liquid Aminos. Set aside for 20 minutes to marinate and soften.

2. Make stock by placing ginger, garlic, bay leaf, and 1 cup water in a blender. Blend until smooth.

3. Add remaining water and the onion marinade mixture. Pulse lightly to mix.

4. Place noodles into four serving bowls. Put vegetables on top of noodles in each bowl. Pour stock into each bowl.

5. Place vegetable garnish onto one plate. Serve as a side along with hoisin sauce.

MAPLE-SCALLION DIPPING SAUCE

MAKES 3 SERVINGS

RECIPE BY LAURA THEODORE

This sweet and rich sauce imparts a bit of an Asian flair that is perfect to pair with tofu, tempeh, or even steamed veggies. The best part is that it uses only three ingredients, but the taste is full-bodied, delicate, and rich.

3 tablespoons maple syrup
1 tablespoon regular or reduced-sodium tamari
1 small scallion, thinly sliced

1. Put the maple syrup and tamari in a small bowl.
2. Whisk to combine.
3. Divide equally into three dipping bowls.
4. Top each serving with some of the sliced scallion.

SHREDDED BRUSSELS SPROUTS & KALE WITH MISO-DIJON SAUCE

MAKES 4+ SERVINGS   RECIPE BY HEATHER CROSBY

One of my favorite quick and easy meals that doesn't taste quick and easy. I often use this recipe as a base and toss in other goodies I have on hand for the week, like carrots, garbanzo beans, and zucchini.

12 brussels sprouts
3–4 large leaves kale, stems removed
2 green onions, sliced
2 teaspoons toasted sesame seeds
Pinch of freshly ground pepper

FOR THE MISO-DIJON SAUCE
1 tablespoon chickpea miso (any light, soy-free, gluten-free miso will do)
1 teaspoon Dijon mustard
2 teaspoons water
¼ teaspoon wasabi powder (optional)
¼ teaspoon dulse flakes (optional)

1. Wash and slice brussels sprouts into strips. If you have a food processor, save time by running your sprouts through the shredder blade. Place in large glass bowl.

2. Wash kale and remove stems. Roll up leaves lengthwise and chiffonade into thin strips (see Tip on page 224).

3. Slice green onion and set aside.

4. In a small bowl, mix together sauce ingredients. Set aside.

5. Heat skillet to medium-high and place sliced onion, shredded kale, and brussels sprouts into pan. Sear veggies for 2–3 minutes and then stir. Sear for another 3 minutes and then stir. Repeat one more time and remove from heat.

6. Fold in sauce and top with sesame seeds and freshly ground pepper. Serve warm.

TIPS

It's best to add the Miso-Dijon Sauce *after* you cook your veggies, since heat destroys the beneficial bacteria that aid digestion and strengthen immunity.

Try adding shredded carrots and/or toasted walnuts to the mix.

Store leftovers in an airtight container in the fridge and reheat on the stovetop.

ALMOND-ENCRUSTED EGGPLANT CUTLETS

MAKES 6 SERVINGS   RECIPE BY CHRISTINA ROSS

1 whole eggplant
1 tablespoon sea salt

FOR THE BREAD CRUMBS
2 cups almonds
4 tablespoons nutritional yeast
¼ teaspoon sea salt
1 tablespoon fresh stemmed rosemary
6 tablespoons flax meal
1 tablespoon sesame seeds
1 teaspoon garlic powder

FOR THE MILK MIXTURE
2 cups almond milk
2 tablespoons fresh thyme
2 tablespoons fresh stemmed rosemary
1 teaspoon black pepper
1 teaspoon Italian seasoning
¼ teaspoon crushed red pepper
2 tablespoons flax meal

1. Preheat oven to 450°F.

2. Slice eggplant into ¼-inch-thick rounds. Place in a bowl and marinate in 1 tablespoon salt until sweaty.

3. Place the bread crumbs ingredients in a food processor and pulse until you achieve coarse bread crumb–like texture.

4. In a shallow bowl, add all milk mixture ingredients and whisk until well combined.

5. Dip each eggplant round in milk mixture and then coat each side with bread crumbs.

6. Set in baking pan lined with parchment paper. Bake for 8 minutes on each side.

7. Remove from oven, plate, and serve.

TIPS

The cutlets are very versatile as they can be eaten as is, made into vegan eggplant Parmesan, or used in a sandwich.

Serve with a side of veggies or salad or over gluten-free pasta.

Store an extra stash of the bread crumbs for future recipes; you can dehydrate them or bake them in the oven and store them in an airtight container. Try breading other vegetables or simply sprinkle the crumbs over your favorite salad.

CAULIFLOWER STEAKS WITH SWEET PEPPER SAUCE

MAKES 6 SERVINGS    RECIPE BY LAURA THEODORE

My husband loves cauliflower. Once he came home from the market with copious amounts of cauliflower and I knew I needed to come up with a new cauliflower recipe . . . and fast! The result is this colorful, impressive, and satisfying entrée that is ideal to serve throughout the fall and winter seasons.

2 medium heads cauliflower
1 red onion, thinly sliced
1 yellow or sweet onion, thinly sliced
2 teaspoons Italian seasoning
1 teaspoon reduced-sodium tamari
¼ cup water, divided, plus more as needed
2 cups cremini or white button mushrooms, thinly sliced

2 sweet red peppers, thinly sliced
1 green pepper, thinly sliced
2 cups jarred, low-fat, oil-free marinara sauce or Dad's Marinara (p. 152), divided, plus more as needed

1. Preheat oven to 375°F.

2. Trim 1–2 inches off two opposite sides of the cauliflower heads and set aside for another use.

3. Steam the trimmed cauliflower heads for 12–18 minutes or until they are just crisp-tender. Cool for 20 minutes.

4. Meanwhile, put the onion, Italian seasoning, tamari, and 2 tablespoons water in a large skillet. Cover and cook over medium heat for 5 minutes, adding more water 1 tablespoon at a time as needed to prevent sticking.

5. Add the mushrooms and cook for 5 minutes.

6. Add the peppers and 2 tablespoons water and continue to cook for 5 minutes.

7. Decrease the heat to medium-low and stir in 1 cup marinara sauce.

8. Cover and let simmer for 8 minutes.

9. Spread 1 cup marinara sauce evenly in the bottom of a rimmed casserole that is large enough to accommodate the cauliflower steaks.

10. Cut each cauliflower head into three ¾–1-inch-thick slices, as if slicing a loaf of bread.

11. Set the cauliflower slices in the prepared casserole and top each with one-sixth of the onion and pepper sauce.

12. Cover and bake 25–35 minutes or until the cauliflower steaks are tender but still firm. Uncover the casserole for the last 10 minutes of cooking time.

13. Cool for 5 minutes. Serve with extra sauce on the side.

POLENTA WITH CHINESE EGGPLANT

MAKES 2 SERVINGS   RECIPE BY CHRISTINA ROSS

5 cloves garlic
1 small onion
1 long Chinese eggplant
1½ cups vegetable stock, divided

Black pepper and sea salt to taste
4 slices precooked polenta
1 12-ounce jar oil-free tomato sauce

1. Peel and mince the garlic and onion.

2. Slice eggplant into ¼-inch-thick rounds.

3. Add sliced eggplant, garlic, onion, and 1 cup vegetable stock to a bowl with pepper and salt to taste. Mix well and pour into heated pan over medium-high heat. Sauté until all liquid is evaporated.

4. Slice precooked polenta into ½-inch-thick rounds.

5. Once liquid has evaporated from pan, scoot eggplant over and add in ¼ cup more stock, followed by the sliced polenta.

6. Cook the polenta on both sides until warmed all the way through and stock has evaporated.

7. Move the polenta over and add remaining ¼ cup stock to the pan over low heat. Add the tomato sauce to the pan and heat until warmed.

8. Remove pan from heat. Ladle tomato sauce onto a plate. Add the polenta in the center of the sauce. Next, using tongs or a fork, place the eggplant on top. Garnish with a fresh herb leaf or flower, if desired, and serve.

TABBOULEH

MAKES 4–6 SERVINGS

½ cup bulgur (see Tip)
1 cup water
1 large cucumber, diced
1½ cups fresh parsley, chopped
2 tablespoons chopped fresh mint
2 cups chopped cherry tomatoes

1 red onion, diced
4 tablespoons fresh lemon juice
Salt to taste
¼ teaspoon black pepper
Pinch of ground nutmeg and allspice
Lettuce

1. Place bulgur and water in a small bowl and let set for 30 minutes.

2. In a separate bowl, mix together cucumber, parsley, mint, tomatoes, onion, lemon juice, salt, black pepper, nutmeg, and allspice.

3. After allowing the bulgur to set for 30 minutes, drain the water and stir bulgur into the cucumber mixture.

4. Cover and refrigerate for 2 hours.

5. Serve tabbouleh on lettuce leaves.

TIP

For those who have a gluten allergy, replace bulgur with 1 cup cooked quinoa.

HURRY CURRY QUINOA SEE PICTURE ON PAGE 139

MAKES 4 SERVINGS    RECIPE BY CHRISTINA ROSS

In a hurry and want some curry? Then I've got just the dish for you. In just under half an hour your taste buds will be teleported to India as you nourish your body with this delicious and warm family-friendly meal.

1 cup quinoa
2½ cups vegetable stock, divided
¼ teaspoon sea salt
1 cup frozen peas
½ zucchini
2 carrots
1 round yellow squash

½ red bell pepper
1 small purple onion
8 slices ginger
½ cup coconut milk
2 tablespoons red curry paste
1 cup chopped fresh cilantro

1. Rinse quinoa in a fine sieve until water runs clear, drain, and transfer to a medium pot.

2. Add 2 cups vegetable stock and ¼ teaspoon salt to the pot and bring to a boil. Cover, decrease heat to medium-low, and let simmer until stock is absorbed, about 15–20 minutes. Set aside off the heat for 5 minutes, then uncover and fluff with a fork.

3. While the quinoa is cooking, prep the veggies for the curry. Thaw the peas. Chop the zucchini, carrots, squash, bell pepper, and purple onion evenly in size.

4. In a separate pan over medium-high heat, add the remaining ½ cup vegetable stock and a pinch of salt to prevent sticking. Once pan is heated, add the onion. Sauté the onion until fragrant and then add the veggies except for the ginger and cilantro. Allow the veggies to cook for a couple of minutes.

5. Add the coconut milk, curry paste, and ginger, stir, and cook on medium heat with lid on until completely warm.

6. Remove from heat and stir in the cilantro. Add the curry to the quinoa pot and mix well. Serve garnished with more cilantro.

COCONUT CURRIED VEGETABLES

MAKES 6–8 SERVINGS    RECIPE BY LEANNE CAMPBELL

1½ cups chopped onion
2 tablespoons vegetable stock
2 tablespoons minced garlic
2 tablespoons minced fresh ginger
1 teaspoon ground turmeric
1 teaspoon ground coriander
1 teaspoon ground cumin
½ teaspoon garam masala
2 cups diced tomatoes

2 tablespoons tomato paste
Sea salt to taste
¼ teaspoon cayenne pepper
4 cups chopped vegetables (combining carrots,
   green beans, peas, summer squash, potatoes)
1 13.5-ounce can lite coconut milk
½ teaspoon fresh lemon juice
4 cups cooked brown rice for serving

1. In a large skillet, sauté onion over medium heat with vegetable stock, stirring frequently, until onion becomes translucent. Stir in garlic, ginger, turmeric, coriander, cumin, and garam masala. Cook for 2 minutes

2. Stir in diced tomatoes, tomato paste, salt, and cayenne pepper, and cook for 3–4 minutes. Stir in vegetables, coconut milk, and lemon juice. Cover and cook for 10–12 minutes on low heat.

3. Serve on top of rice.

THAI PINEAPPLE CURRY

MAKES 2 SERVINGS   RECIPE BY LINDSAY NIXON

This curry has just the right sweet-to-heat ratio and is bursting with Thai flavors.

4 green onions, sliced
1 tablespoon minced ginger
2–3 cloves garlic, minced
¼ cup vegetable stock
1 red bell pepper, seeded and sliced into thin strips
½–1 red finger pepper, seeded and sliced
Crushed red pepper to taste (optional)

1 8-ounce can diced pineapple (in juice, not syrup)
1¼ teaspoons mild yellow curry powder
½ cup lite coconut milk
2 tablespoons minced fresh basil
½ teaspoon low-sodium soy sauce
Lime wedges for garnish

1. Set aside a few dark green onion slices for garnish. Transfer the rest of the onions to a skillet with ginger and garlic.

2. Add enough stock so there is a thin lining on the bottom of the skillet and sauté over high heat for 1–2 minutes until onion, ginger, and garlic are fragrant.

3. Add red bell pepper and red finger pepper (or crushed red pepper as desired) and sauté until bell peppers start to soften, adding splashes of stock as necessary to prevent sticking.

4. Once bell peppers start to soften, add pineapple with juices, stirring to combine.

5. Cook for another minute until peppers are cooked but still somewhat crisp and pineapple is warm.

6. Meanwhile, in a measuring cup or small bowl, whisk curry powder into coconut milk, then pour into skillet and stir to combine.

7. After 30 seconds, add basil and soy sauce, stirring again to combine. Taste, adding more soy sauce or basil if desired.

8. Garnish with green onions, lime wedges, and 1–2 basil leaves.

TIPS

For a complete meal, add cubed tofu and serve over cooked brown rice.

For a lower-fat version, replace half of the coconut milk with sweetened nondairy milk or use all nondairy milk with a drop of coconut extract.

PINEAPPLE NOT-SO-FRIED RICE

MAKES 4–6 SERVINGS    RECIPE BY CHRISTY MORGAN

I love fried rice, but I don't love all the oil it uses. I came up with this healthier oil-free version that is very similar to the fried rice I used to get at Chinese restaurants growing up.

1 cup brown or white basmati rice
1 cup frozen peas, defrosted
1 14-ounce can pineapple chunks, juice
   reserved
1 cup diced carrot

½ cup asparagus, cut on diagonal
2 tablespoons tamari or to taste
½ cup cilantro leaves, packed (optional)
Sea salt and black pepper to taste
Toasted sesame seeds for garnish

1. Cook rice according to package instructions. When rice is done, place in a medium bowl with peas.

2. Meanwhile, bring pineapple juice to a boil and simmer pineapple chunks, carrot, asparagus, and tamari until veggies are tender but still crunchy, about 5 minutes.

3. Toss with rice and cilantro, if using, and season with salt and pepper to taste.

4. Garnish with toasted sesame seeds and serve.

VEGGIE UNFRIED JICAMA RICE

MAKES 6 SERVINGS

RECIPE BY CHRISTINA ROSS

This dish is perfect for those warm summer lunches since you don't even need to turn on the stove. The juicy jicama lends a crisp sweet taste, making it the perfect rice substitute, and when paired with ginger and tamari this Mexican vegetable takes on an Asian flair.

FOR THE RICE
1 large jicama
½ cup cashews
3 tablespoons agave
1½ tablespoons coconut nectar
1 teaspoon sea salt
1 teaspoon black pepper

FOR THE VEGGIES
¼ cup purple onion
¼ cup purple cabbage
4 stems green onion
2 medium carrots
1 stalk celery
¼ cup broccoli
¼ cup portobello or shiitake mushrooms

FOR THE DRESSING
1 small ginger nugget
3 cloves garlic
1 orange, juiced
¼ cup tamari
1 tablespoon agave
½ teaspoon black pepper
¼ teaspoon crushed red pepper to taste
1 tablespoon flax seeds

1. To make the "rice," peel the jicama using a vegetable peeler and then roughly chop into cubes.

2. Add all rice ingredients into your food processor and pulse until you achieve a rice texture. Be sure to not overprocess or your rice will turn to mush.

3. Empty the rice into a large serving bowl and set aside.

4. Dice all veggies evenly into small pieces and place in medium mixing bowl.

5. Prep veggies for the dressing. Peel the ginger with a paring knife or vegetable peeler. Peel the garlic and remove the inner green stem. Juice the orange.

6. Add all dressing ingredients except for the flax seeds to a blender and blend until smooth.

7. Pour the dressing over the veggies and stir. Let the veggies marinate for a few minutes, stirring occasionally, and then sprinkle flax seeds on top.

8. Pour the marinated veggies over the jicama rice and fold them in until well combined. Serve with chopsticks.

WALNUT CRANBERRY SQUASH "RICE"

MAKES 4 SERVINGS

RECIPE BY ANI PHYO

Cranberries are packed with antioxidants and promote a healthy heart, teeth, gums, and urinary tract. They help fight cancer and may help prevent stomach ulcers.

1 small butternut squash (about 1 pound), peeled, seeded, and cut into 2-inch cubes
½ small yellow onion, chopped (about ½ cup)
1 tablespoon cumin seeds
1 tablespoon coriander powder

½ cup fresh cilantro leaves, chopped
1 cup dried cranberries
1 cup walnuts, crushed
2 teaspoons sea salt

1. Put small batches of cubed squash in a food processor and process into small pieces.
2. Put processed squash in a large mixing bowl. Add onion, cumin, coriander, cilantro, cranberries, walnuts, and salt, and mix well.

TIPS

A potato peeler works great for peeling the skin off squash. Once peeled, cut squash in half lengthwise and remove the seeds. Then cut it into smaller pieces.

If cranberries are hard to find, you can also use raisins or dates instead.

Serve with Coconut Chutney (p. 215) and a soup or salad on the side.

This dish will keep for 2 days in the fridge.

RICE AND BEANS

MAKES 8–10 SERVINGS

RECIPE BY JOHN AND MARY MCDOUGALL

Some days we are in the mood for a simple, healthy rice and bean meal. This delicious dish cooks in one pot, has lots of flavor, and can be eaten plain, topped with salsa or hot sauce, or rolled up in a tortilla.

1 onion, chopped
2 cloves garlic, minced
½ cup vegetable stock
4½ cups water
2 cups long grain brown rice
3 15-ounce cans pinto beans, drained and rinsed

2 4-ounce cans chopped green chilies
1 teaspoon ground cumin
¼–½ teaspoon crushed red pepper
Sea salt to taste (optional)

1. Place the onion, garlic, and vegetable stock in a large saucepan.

2. Cook, stirring frequently, until onion softens slightly, about 3 minutes.

3. Add the remaining ingredients except for salt, mix well, and bring to a boil.

4. Decrease heat, cover, and let simmer for about 45 minutes until rice is tender and liquid has been absorbed.

5. Mix gently before serving. Season with a bit of salt before serving, if desired.

TIPS

This recipe may also be made with black or small red beans.

Enjoy leftovers for lunch the next day or freeze half of this recipe for later use.

OMEGA-3 FATTY ACIDS

What's the big deal about omega-3 fatty acids? As stated in *Whole*, "Omega-3 fatty acids are one of the current darlings of the mainstream nutritional health world. To ensure we get enough of them, the media urges us to eat lots of fish, specifically fatty species like anchovies, herring, salmon, sardines, and tuna. They don't often mention that one form of omega-3, ALA, which is found in certain nuts and seeds, can be converted in the body into the other forms, making fish consumption unnecessary."*

Whole, p. 159

BEAN LOAF

MAKES 8 SERVINGS   RECIPE BY JOHN AND MARY MCDOUGALL

5 cups cooked beans (any kind)
1 cup cooked brown rice
1 onion, chopped
1 green pepper, chopped
1 cup chopped celery
1 clove garlic, crushed
1½ cups tomato sauce
2 tablespoons bran

1 teaspoon dried basil
1 teaspoon dried oregano
2 teaspoons chili powder
1 teaspoon ground cumin
¼ teaspoon cayenne (optional)
1 tablespoon parsley flakes
1 tablespoon low-sodium soy sauce (optional)
2 tablespoons cornmeal

1. Preheat oven to 350°F.

2. Mash the beans and combine them with the rice. Set aside.

3. Sauté the onion, green pepper, celery, and garlic in ⅓ cup water for 5 minutes. Add to the bean mixture.

4. Add all of the remaining ingredients, except the cornmeal, and mix well.

5. Sprinkle the cornmeal over the bottom of a 9 × 5 × 3 nonstick loaf pan.

6. Place the bean mixture in the pan, smoothing out the top. Bake for 45 minutes.

TIP

This makes a delicious sandwich spread when cold.

LAYERED BEAN CASSEROLE

MAKES 6 SERVINGS    RECIPE BY JOHN AND MARY MCDOUGALL

FOR THE BOTTOM LAYER

1 15-ounce can black beans, drained and
   rinsed
1 15-ounce can red or pinto beans, drained
   and rinsed
1 15-ounce can chili beans in oil-free sauce,
   undrained
1 8-ounce can tomato sauce
1 cup frozen corn kernels, thawed slightly
¼ cup chopped onion
2 teaspoons chili powder

FOR THE MIDDLE LAYER

1 15-ounce can white beans, drained and
   rinsed
½ cup fresh salsa
⅓ cup nutritional yeast
2 tablespoons fresh lemon juice
1 teaspoon granulated onion
1 teaspoon prepared yellow mustard

FOR THE TOP LAYER

1 20-ounce bag fresh shredded oil-free hash
   brown potatoes

1. Preheat oven to 375°F.

2. Mix all ingredients for the bottom layer together and ladle into the bottom of a
   9 × 13 baking dish, distributing evenly.

3. Place all ingredients for the middle layer in a food processor and process until very
   smooth. Pour over the bean layer and spread evenly.

4. Sprinkle the potatoes evenly over the bottom two layers. Bake uncovered for
   45 minutes until potatoes are brown and sauce is bubbly.

TIPS

Serve with hot sauce to drizzle over the top for more heat or serve with tofu sour cream
to mellow it out a bit.

This recipe can be prepared ahead and then popped into the oven just before dinner.

CHEF AJ'S DISAPPEARING LASAGNA

MAKES 12–16 SLICES  RECIPE BY CHEF AJ

People always ask me how well this freezes. I honestly don't know since there have never been any leftovers!

2 15-ounce cans cannellini beans, drained and rinsed

2 cups fresh basil leaves, fully packed

2 cloves garlic or more to taste

¼ cup fresh lemon juice

¼ cup low-sodium miso

¼ cup nutritional yeast

1 cup pine nuts, raw cashews, or hemp seeds

⅛ teaspoon crushed red pepper or more to taste

2 pounds chopped frozen spinach or kale (defrosted and drained with all of the liquid squeezed out)

1 large red onion, finely diced

4 cloves garlic, minced

2 pounds sliced mushrooms (I prefer cremini or baby bellas)

¼ cup low-sodium tamari or raw coconut aminos

6 cups oil-free marinara sauce, divided

2 boxes no-boil rice lasagna noodles (I prefer DeBoles)

1 4-ounce can sliced olives, drained and rinsed (optional)

Faux Parmesan (p. 196) for sprinkling

1. Make the filling in a food processor by combining the beans, basil, garlic, lemon juice, miso, nutritional yeast, nuts or hemp seeds, and crushed red pepper. Puree until smooth.

2. Add drained spinach or kale and process again.

3. In a large nonstick sauté pan, sauté the onion in 2 tablespoons water until translucent, about 8 minutes, adding more water if necessary.

4. Add garlic, mushrooms, and tamari and sauté until browned. Cook until mushrooms appear to be glazed and there is no more liquid left in the pan.

5. Pour 3 cups marinara sauce in a lasagna pan or a 9 × 13 pan.

6. Place a layer of the no-cook noodles on top. Cover the noodles with half of the tofu-spinach mixture, then with half of the mushroom mixture.

7. Place another layer of noodles on the mushroom mixture and add the remaining half of the tofu-spinach mixture and the remaining half of the mushroom mixture.

8. Place one more layer of noodles on top of the mushroom mixture and smother evenly with the remaining 3 cups sauce.

9. Sprinkle the sliced olives on top of the sauce along with a liberal sprinkling of Faux Parmesan (p. 196).

10. Bake uncovered in a preheated 375°F oven for 1 hour. Let set 10 minutes before slicing.

TIPS

If you have time, marinate the sliced mushrooms in the tamari several hours in advance or even the night before.

Make sure that the top layer of noodles is fully covered with sauce.

FAUX PARMESAN

MAKES 1½ CUPS

RECIPE BY CHEF AJ

This is much more economical than the store-bought version.

1 cup raw almonds, cashews, or walnuts
½ cup nutritional yeast
1 tablespoon sodium-free seasoning (I prefer Benson's Table Tasty)

1. In a food processor or blender, combine all ingredients until a powdery texture is achieved.

2. If you like it chunkier, process less.

> **TIPS**
>
> You can also use store-bought almond flour in place of the almonds.
>
> Try serving with air-popped popcorn, potatoes, or steamed veggies, and use as a topping on chili and soups.

ENCHILADA STRATA

MAKES 16 SLICES    RECIPE BY CHEF AJ

FOR THE SAUCE
1 red onion, chopped
2 cloves garlic, crushed
1½ cups water
1 28-ounce can sodium-free tomatoes, fire roasted preferred
2 tablespoons sodium-free chili powder
1 teaspoon roasted cumin
3 tablespoons arrowroot powder

FOR THE FILLING
2½ pounds sweet potatoes
4 cups sodium-free salsa
1 pound bag frozen roasted corn, defrosted
2 15-ounce cans of sodium-free black beans, drained and rinsed, or 6 cups cooked beans
2 16-ounce bags of frozen kale, defrosted with all of the liquid squeezed out
1 4-ounce can mild green chilies
12 corn tortillas, divided
Sliced olives and scallions (optional)

1. Preheat oven to 350°F.

2. Place the onion, garlic, and water in a pot and cook for 8–10 minutes until soft.

3. Stir in tomatoes and spices and cook on low heat for 15 minutes.

4. Add the arrowroot powder to a small amount of cold water and dissolve, then add to sauce and stir until thickened.

5. Peel sweet potatoes and boil or steam until soft.

6. Process potatoes in a food processor until smooth and creamy.

7. Place mashed sweet potatoes into a large bowl and stir in the salsa, corn, beans, kale, and green chilies. Mix well. I recommend using food service gloves so that everything gets fully incorporated.

8. Cover the bottom of a large baking dish with half of the enchilada sauce. A lasagna pan (10 × 14 or 11 × 15) is recommended.

9. Place 6 tortillas on top of the enchilada sauce and then gently and evenly place the sweet potato mixture on top of the tortillas.

10. Top with the remaining 6 tortillas. Pour the remaining sauce over the tortillas and sprinkle sliced olives, if using, over the top.

11. Bake for 30 minutes. Sprinkle with scallions, if using, and serve with hummus guacamole.

SIDE DISHES

ALMOND-CREAMED CAULIFLOWER

MAKES 4–5 SERVINGS

RECIPE BY LEANNE CAMPBELL

1 head cauliflower, chopped and cooked
½ cup vegetable stock
1 cup unsweetened almond milk

1 teaspoon crushed garlic
2 tablespoons cornmeal
Salt and pepper to taste

1. Chop and cook the cauliflower in vegetable stock.

2. In separate pan, mix milk, garlic, and cornmeal. Add cooked cauliflower.

3. Bring to a slow boil, cooking constantly until thick, about 5 minutes.

4. Add salt and pepper to taste.

5. Serve immediately.

THE CHINA STUDY ALL-STAR COLLECTION

ASPARAGUS WITH VEGAN HOLLANDAISE SAUCE

MAKES 4–6 SERVINGS   RECIPE BY LAURA THEODORE

Asparagus is one of the first crops of spring. Paired with rich-tasting vegan "hollandaise" sauce, it makes the perfect vegetable side dish for any special meal.

1 large bunch asparagus, trimmed
3 tablespoons fresh lemon juice
8 ounces soft silken or regular tofu, drained

¼ teaspoon turmeric
¼ teaspoon sea salt

1. Fit a steamer basket into a medium saucepan with a tight-fitting lid. Add 2 inches of cold water, then add the asparagus. Cover and bring to a boil. Steam the asparagus for 4–6 minutes or just until crisp-tender.

2. Meanwhile, put the lemon juice, tofu, turmeric, and salt in a blender and process until smooth.

3. Transfer to a small saucepan and cook over low heat, stirring constantly, until heated through.

4. Arrange the hot asparagus on a serving platter and pour the sauce over top. Serve immediately.

BABY BOK CHOY WITH CHINESE CABBAGE IN GINGER SAUCE

MAKES 4 SERVINGS   RECIPE BY ANI PHYO

Napa cabbage comes from the Beijing region of China, is often used in East Asian cuisine, and is also called Chinese cabbage. Bok choy is a type of Chinese cabbage with dark green leaves, a sweet taste, and a crisp texture. Hong Kong supposedly has over twenty varieties of bok choy. We like to think "bigger is better" in the West, but the smaller version known as Shanghai or baby bok choy is desired for its tenderness in the East.

2 cups sliced baby bok choy, ends trimmed and cut diagonally into 1½-inch strips
1 cup thinly sliced Napa cabbage

FOR THE GINGER SAUCE
3 tablespoons Nama Shoyu
2 tablespoons apple cider vinegar
2 tablespoons agave syrup
1½ teaspoons grated ginger
1 tablespoon chopped scallion

1. Place sliced bok choy and Napa cabbage into mixing bowl. Set aside.

2. To make sauce, whisk together Nama Shoyu, vinegar, agave syrup, and ginger in a small bowl.

3. Pour over bok choy and cabbage and toss to mix well. Set aside for at least 15–30 minutes to soften and marinate.

4. To serve, transfer into a serving dish. Garnish with scallion.

TIPS

If baby bok choy is unavailable, you can use the larger bok choy variety instead.

This recipe will keep for 1 day in the fridge.

CUMIN & PINK PEPPERCORN ROASTED CARROTS

MAKES 4+ SERVINGS

RECIPE BY HEATHER CROSBY

Cumin, fresh orange, and the citrus notes of pink peppercorn take these carrots to the next level of deliciousness.

1 pound small carrots
¼ teaspoon ground cumin
2 tablespoons vegetable stock
1 teaspoon navel or blood orange zest

3 tablespoons fresh navel or blood orange juice
Fresh cracked pink peppercorn
Fine ground sea salt to taste

1. Preheat oven to 350°F.
2. Wash carrots, leave peel on, and slice in half lengthwise.
3. In a small bowl, whisk together cumin, vegetable stock, orange zest, and juice.
4. Place carrots into baking dish and pour cumin mixture over carrots.
5. Season with a pinch of salt and generously sprinkle with fresh cracked pink peppercorn.
6. Roast for 30 minutes. Serve warm.

TIPS

Try adding other root veggies like beets, parsnips, and sweet potatoes to the mix.

These carrots also make a tasty topping for a fresh green salad. Just dice chilled leftovers and toss with greens, sunflower seeds, sesame seeds, walnuts, sprouts, and a squeeze of lemon or orange juice.

STEAMED GREEN BEANS AND CARROTS WITH ORANGE SAUCE

MAKES 4 SERVINGS

RECIPE BY LAURA THEODORE

The refreshing citrus notes of the orange juice enhance this colorful green beans and carrots combo.

4 carrots, scrubbed and sliced into sticks
3 cups green beans, cleaned and trimmed
2 tablespoons orange juice

1 tablespoon fresh lemon juice
1 teaspoon maple syrup
Sesame seeds for garnish

1. Fit a steamer basket into a large saucepan with a tight-fitting lid. Add 2 inches of cold water, then add the carrots. Cover and bring to a boil. Steam for 5 minutes.

2. Add the green beans, cover, and steam for 6–7 minutes more or until the carrots and beans are crisp-tender.

3. Meanwhile, put the orange juice, lemon juice, and maple syrup in a small bowl. Whisk to combine.

4. Transfer the cooked carrots and beans to a medium bowl. Add the sauce, toss to coat, and serve.

LEMON-KISSED BRUSSELS AND BUTTERNUT SQUASH

MAKES 4–6 SERVINGS   RECIPE BY CHRISTY MORGAN

I know so many people who think they don't like brussels sprouts, but after trying this dish, they realize they just haven't had them cooked well. If you think you are a brussels hater, try this dish immediately!

1 butternut squash, peeled and cut into ½-inch cubes (about 3 cups)

2 cups brussels sprouts, halved and ends trimmed

⅓ cup slivered almonds

1 teaspoon grated ginger

1 tablespoon lemon zest

1 tablespoon fresh lemon juice

1 tablespoon tamari

1 tablespoon maple or brown rice syrup

1 tablespoon brown rice vinegar or other vinegar

Sea salt to taste

1. Steam butternut squash until just tender. Place in a medium bowl.

2. Steam brussels sprouts until just tender and place in bowl with squash.

3. Pan-toast almonds in a skillet over a medium-low heat until golden brown, stirring continuously.

4. Mix together the rest of the ingredients in a small bowl, then toss with veggies and almonds until well combined. Season with salt to taste.

QUICK CURRIED POTATOES

MAKES 3–4 SERVINGS

RECIPE BY LEANNE CAMPBELL

2 medium potatoes, diced and cooked
⅓ cup coconut milk
2 teaspoons crushed garlic
¼ teaspoon black pepper

¼ teaspoon fresh lemon juice
1 tablespoon curry powder
¼ teaspoon sea salt
¼ teaspoon raw sugar

1. In a small saucepan, cook diced potatoes.
2. In a skillet, add cooked potatoes, coconut milk, garlic, black pepper, lemon juice, curry powder, salt, and sugar. Cook for 5–7 minutes over medium-high heat. Serve immediately.

NUMBERS AND FIGURES

If you're just beginning to eat a whole foods, plant-based diet (WFPB) and you're worried about precise formulas and rules—how many ounces of leafy greens should you eat daily, what proportion of your diet should be fat, protein, or carbohydrate, etc.—don't be! When Dr. Campbell lectures publicly, he's often asked about the numbers, but as he explains in *Whole*, "Relax. When it comes to numbers, I am reluctant to be too precise, mostly because (1) we don't yet have scientific evidence that fully answers these questions; (2) virtually nothing in biology is as precise as we try to make it seem; and (3) as far as the evidence suggests at this point, eating the WFPB way eliminates the need to worry about the details. Just eat lots of different plant foods; your body will do all the math for you!"*

Whole, p. 11

5-MINUTE CRANBERRY RELISH

MAKES 4 CUPS   RECIPE BY CHEF AJ

Why cook your relish or use sugar when you can make this instead? This relish is delicious served with oatmeal.

1 12-ounce bag fresh cranberries
2 large peeled oranges, zest included
Dates to taste

2 tablespoons psyllium husk
Fresh ginger (optional)
Fresh lime juice (optional)

1. In a food processor, process all of the ingredients until the desired chunky texture is reached.

2. Adding fresh ginger and lime juice is also a delicious variation.

COCONUT CHUTNEY

MAKES 4 SERVINGS

RECIPE BY ANI PHYO

Packed with electrolytes, this chutney is a great addition to any dish. Try it alongside the Walnut Cranberry Squash "Rice" (p. 187).

Coconut meat from 2–3 Thai baby coconuts
  (about 1 cup), chopped, divided
½ lemon, juiced (about 1 tablespoon)
1 clove garlic, minced

1 small Thai red chili pepper
½ cup cilantro leaves, chopped
¼ cup yellow onion, chopped
½ teaspoon sea salt

1. Blend ¼ cup coconut meat with lemon juice.
2. Put coconut mixture, remaining coconut meat, garlic, chili, cilantro, onion, and salt in a bowl. Mix well.

DAIKON KIMCHI SEE PICTURE ON PAGE 199

MAKES ABOUT 2 QUARTS OR ½ GALLON

RECIPE BY ANI PHYO

Korean radish is also known as *tae baek* or *moo* in Korean. It's large, about 6 inches long, and has a green tip. It's found in China and Thailand, as well as in Korea.

1 teaspoon minced garlic

1 tablespoon grated ginger

½ tablespoon Korean chili powder or
 ½ teaspoon cayenne powder, more or
 less to taste

½ tablespoon sea salt

½ tablespoon agave syrup

8 cups cubed daikon (from about ½ large
 daikon), peeled and cut into 1-inch cubes

½ cup sliced scallion, cut in 1-inch lengths

1. In a food processor or using a mortar and pestle, mince or grind together garlic, ginger, chili powder or cayenne, and salt.

2. Add agave syrup and mix well to a paste-like consistency.

3. Place radish and scallion into a mixing bowl. Wearing gloves, coat daikon evenly with the garlic mixture.

4. Pack radish into a ½-gallon glass jar or two 1-quart mason jars and seal the lid tightly. Set jar in a cool, dark cabinet for 3–4 days to pickle and ferment.

5. Refrigerate after opening. Will keep for a couple weeks in fridge.

> **TIP**
>
> For a better flavor, ideally, you'll want to use a Korean radish. Look for it in Asian grocery stores or buy seeds and grow your own. Korean radish is slightly different from daikon. It's stubbier and more round, while the daikon is longer. Daikon is more common, however.

MOCK TUNA

MAKES 6–8 SERVINGS   RECIPE BY CHRISTY MORGAN

You will be shocked at how delicious this mock tuna is without all the saturated fat that comes with the real thing. Walnuts are used in place of tuna for their rich omega-3 content. Sea vegetables like kelp and dulse are used to give a hint of fish flavor while adding nutrient-rich trace minerals to the dish.

1 cup almonds, soaked 4 hours
½ cup walnuts, soaked 4 hours
2 carrots, grated
2 stalks celery, minced
1 lemon, juiced
1 lime, juiced
3 tablespoons kelp granules

2 tablespoons dulse flakes
2 tablespoons nutritional yeast
2 tablespoons dried parsley
1 teaspoon maple syrup or brown rice syrup
1 teaspoon coriander
3 tablespoons tamari
¼ cup water, more or less as needed

1. Drain nuts, then blend in a food processor until finely ground.

2. Add the rest of the ingredients and blend until almost smooth. Be sure to scrape down the edges of the bowl a few times to incorporate all the ingredients.

3. Serve with crackers or pita bread.

JICAMA SLAW WITH CREAMY POPPY SEED DRESSING

MAKES 6–8 SERVINGS

RECIPE BY DEL SROUFE

Crisp, clean-tasting jicama gets dressed up with this delicious poppy seed dressing. This slaw makes a great filling for wraps with hummus.

2 tablespoons agave nectar or brown rice syrup
2 tablespoons rice wine vinegar
1 tablespoon poppy seeds
½ tablespoon Dijon mustard
½ teaspoon onion powder
¼ teaspoon sea salt

¾ cup firm silken tofu (about half of a 12-ounce package)
6 cups grated jicama
1 medium carrot, grated
6 green onions, thinly sliced

1. To make the dressing, combine the agave nectar or brown rice syrup, rice wine vinegar, poppy seeds, Dijon mustard, onion powder, salt, and silken tofu in a food processor or a blender, and puree until smooth and creamy.

2. Add the remaining ingredients to a bowl with the dressing and mix well.

3. Refrigerate until ready to serve.

CILANTRO-LIME SLAW

RECIPE BY DEL SROUFE

I love this slaw with Adzuki Bean Tacos (p. 132). The tangy, spicy slaw contrasts nicely with the almost-sweet adzuki beans in the tacos.

4 cups coleslaw mix
½ cup chopped fresh cilantro
1 jalapeño pepper, minced (optional)
1 lime, zested and juiced

4 tablespoons brown rice vinegar, more or less to taste
Sea salt to taste

1. Combine all ingredients in a bowl and mix well.

BREAD CRUMBS

Can't find whole-wheat bread crumbs at the store? No problem. All you need is a food processor, a pan, and this trio of steps.

1 slice whole-wheat bread

1. Tear bread into equal pieces.
2. Place in a food processor. Allow the motor to run until the bread is shredded and crumbs result.
3. Place in a single layer on a pan and allow to air out and become stale (should be hard and crunchy).

> **TIP**
>
> If you're in a hurry, toast crumbs in a convenrional oven or toaster oven for a few minutes at 250°F.

AFRICAN COLLARD STIR-FRY

MAKES 3–5 SERVINGS    RECIPE BY CHRISTY MORGAN

I love Southern comfort-style collard greens, but most of the time the dish is full of oil and fat, and the greens are cooked until there is no life left in them. This is my healthier, more vibrant version with a touch of orange.

½ cup water
2 cups matchstick-cut sweet potatoes
Pinch of sea salt
⅓ cup orange juice
1 tablespoon peanut butter
2 tablespoons tamari

½ teaspoon curry powder
½ cup matchstick-cut carrot
2 tablespoons raisins (optional)
1 bunch collards, stems removed, leaves in
    chiffonade (see Tip), 4 stems thinly sliced on
    diagonal

1. Heat water in a medium skillet. When water boils, add sweet potato and salt, cover with lid, and simmer for three to five minutes.

2. Meanwhile, whisk together juice, peanut butter, tamari, and curry powder.

3. Add carrots, raisins, if using, and collards with sauce mix in skillet.

4. Let simmer for 3–5 minutes until all the veggies are tender but not mushy.

5. Stir occasionally to coat the greens with the sauce.

TIP

A chiffonade is a fine slice or shred of leafy vegetables or herbs. To chiffonade, simply stack a few leaves, roll them into a cigar shape, and slice. Remember to remove any tough, woody stems that you want to exclude from your preparation.

GINGERED COLLARD GREENS

MAKES 2 SERVINGS   RECIPE BY LINDSAY NIXON

This is one of my favorite Ethiopian dishes. Although I normally like to drown my collard greens in hot sauce, a local Ethiopian restaurant showed me how fresh ginger really complements the greens' unique taste.

Pinch of crushed red pepper

2 cloves garlic, minced

⅓ cup finely chopped red onion

2 tablespoons minced fresh ginger

2 cups chopped collard greens

Salt and pepper to taste

Hot sauce (optional)

1. Line a large pot with a thin layer of water—the thinnest layer possible. Bring to a boil and sauté a good pinch of crushed red pepper for 30 seconds.

2. Add garlic and onion and cook for another minute.

3. Add ginger and then collards, using tongs or a spatula to flip and move the greens around. Add splashes of water as necessary and continue to cook until the collards are bright green, or cook them longer if you prefer a well-cooked and soft green.

4. Season generously with salt and pepper.

5. Give it a good stir and serve with hot sauce on the table.

TIP

You can also substitute any greens you like here, but I like collard greens the best.

MUSTARD GREENS

MAKES 4–6 SERVINGS

I often make a pot of greens to have on hand. Frequently they end up in a bowl over rice and beans, served with hot pepper or a little nutritional yeast.

4 pounds mustard greens, stemmed and
    washed
1 large onion, diced

2 cloves garlic, minced
Sea salt and black pepper to taste

1. Bring a large pot of water to a boil, add the mustard greens in batches, and let them cook for 5 minutes.

2. Remove the greens from the water and transfer them to a large bowl with ice water to stop their cooking and help them retain their color.

3. Sauté the onion in a large skillet for 7–8 minutes over medium heat. Add water 1–2 tablespoons at a time to keep the onion from sticking.

4. Add the garlic and cook for another minute.

5. Add the greens and cook for 5 minutes. Season with salt and pepper.

> **TIP**
>
> If you want to make this dish with quick-cooking arugula or spinach, skip the part where you cook the greens in boiling water. Instead, cook them, covered, with the sautéed onion and garlic for a few minutes and then season with salt and pepper.

RAINBOW GREENS

MAKES 2 SERVINGS   RECIPE BY LINDSAY NIXON

I've always been attracted to rainbow chard (it's just so pretty!) but taste-wise it was my least favorite green, until I thought to pair it with raisins. The raisins add a nice sweetness to the dish, which helps mellow the earthy and sometimes bitter flavor chard can have.

1 bunch rainbow chard (see Tips)   **1 teaspoon apple cider vinegar**
4 cloves garlic, minced   **¼ cup raisins**
Pinch of dried oregano   **Salt and pepper to taste**

1. Coarsely chop well-rinsed chard, and set aside.

2. Line a large pot or skillet with a thin layer of water.

3. Add garlic, oregano, and vinegar and bring to a boil, sautéing garlic over high heat for a minute.

4. Add raisins and cook for another minute, then add chard. Use tongs or a spatula to stir chard around so it cooks down and incorporates with the other ingredients.

5. Once chard is softer and brighter in color, turn off heat and mix everything well.

6. Season with salt and pepper and serve.

TIPS

If you don't have access to chard, no problem! Any sturdy greens, like collards or kale, are a fine substitute.

Although I remove the stems from most leafy greens, I leave them intact here. If you use collards or kale, you'll want to cut away the stems.

To turn this dish into a full meal, toss in garbanzo beans and serve with a grain such as quinoa or couscous.

PARSNIP MASHED POTATOES

MAKES 4 SERVINGS

RECIPE BY DEL SROUFE

Parsnips add a little zing to otherwise-ordinary mashed potatoes. They also make them a little creamier. While I normally pass over mashed potatoes as a side dish, I can eat a bowlful of this tasty version.

6 medium red or white new potatoes, cubed
3 medium parsnips, peeled and cubed

Dash of cayenne pepper
1 teaspoon sea salt

1. Put the potatoes and parsnips in a large pot with just enough water to cover the vegetables. Bring to a boil, decrease heat to medium, and then cover and let simmer for 20–30 minutes, stirring occasionally with a spoon.

2. Test the tenderness of the potatoes and parsnips with a fork; they should pierce easily and be tender yet firm.

3. Drain any remaining liquid and mash the potatoes and parsnips with a potato masher until there are no visible lumps.

4. Gently stir in the cayenne pepper and salt with a wooden spoon.

TWICE-BAKED STUFFED SWEET POTATOES

MAKES 8 SERVINGS RECIPE BY CHEF AJ

This dish is so pretty and tastes as good as it looks. It's a great way to use your leftover cranberry relish.

4–5 medium sweet potatoes
½ cup 5-Minute Cranberry Relish (p. 214)

½ cup dried unsweetened cranberries
½ cup pecans (optional)

1. Microwave sweet potatoes until tender. Cool slightly and then cut in half. Scoop pulp from each potato half leaving about a ¼-inch border so that the potato halves will stand up and can be filled.

2. Mash sweet potatoes with a potato masher and add cranberry relish and dried cranberries. Mix well to combine.

3. Scoop potato mixture evenly into potato shells. Sprinkle with pecans, if desired.

4. Bake in a 350°F preheated oven for 30 minutes or until heated through.

TWICE-BAKED POTATOES

MAKES 6 SERVINGS   RECIPE BY LAURA THEODORE

Both my grandma and my mom often made twice-baked potatoes and I just loved them! Because it was one of my favorite dishes as a child, I set out to create an equally delectable spud, stuffed with a smooth and savory filling that is reminiscent of childhood culinary bliss!

3 very large russet potatoes, scrubbed, baked, and cooled (see Tip)

1 cup cooked white beans (drained and rinsed if using canned beans)

¼ cup nondairy milk, plus more as needed

⅛ teaspoon garlic powder

⅛ teaspoon sea salt or Himalayan pink salt, plus more as needed

2 tablespoons minced onion

2 tablespoons diced sweet red pepper

½ teaspoon paprika

¼ teaspoon Italian seasoning

Freshly ground pepper to taste

1. Preheat oven to 375°F. Line a small, rimmed baking pan with unbleached parchment paper.

2. Slice each potato in half lengthwise. Carefully scoop out the pulp, using a teaspoon or grapefruit spoon, leaving about ¼ inch of the potato skin and pulp intact.

3. Put the potato pulp, white beans, nondairy milk, garlic powder, and ⅛ teaspoon salt in a high-performance blending appliance and process until smooth. If the mixture is still lumpy, add more nondairy milk, 1 tablespoon at a time, to achieve a smooth consistency.

4. Put the potato mixture in a medium bowl. Gently stir in the onion and pepper.

5. Using a large spoon or piping bag, spoon or pipe ⅙ of the potato mixture into each potato skin.

6. Place the potato on the prepared baking pan. Repeat until all of the potato skins are filled.

7. Sprinkle the tops of each potato with paprika, Italian seasoning, salt, and pepper to taste.

8. Tent the baking pan with foil and bake for 40 minutes. Uncover and bake for 15–20 minutes or until the tops are crispy and slightly golden. Let cool for 5–7 minutes and serve.

TIP

The russet potatoes may be baked up to 24 hours in advance of preparing this recipe. After they have cooled, wrap them tightly in foil and store them in the refrigerator until use.

BAKED ONION RINGS

I daresay I like these better than the greasy, deep-fried kind.

1 large Vidalia onion
½ cup Bread Crumbs (p. 221)
½ cup yellow cornmeal
1 teaspoon fine salt, plus more as needed

1 teaspoon granulated onion powder
1 teaspoon granulated garlic powder
½ cup chickpea flour
½ cup nondairy milk

1. Preheat oven to 400°F. Line a large baking sheet with parchment paper and set aside.

2. Cut onion into ⅓-inch-thick rings, reserving all large and medium rings, about 30–40 rings, and store the smaller pieces for another use.

3. Grind down bread crumbs and cornmeal in mortar and pestle into a fine sand-like consistency.

4. Whisk bread crumb–cornmeal mixture, salt, and spices together in a bowl and set aside.

5. Pour chickpea flour in another bowl and nondairy milk in a third bowl.

6. Place the bowls together in a triangle, with the nondairy milk bowl pointing at you in the center.

7. Fully dip an onion ring in the nondairy milk, twirl it in chickpea flour until coated, then quickly dip back into the nondairy milk and immediately dredge in crumb mixture until evenly coated.

8. Place on cookie sheet and repeat with all rings.

9. Bake for 10–15 minutes until crisp and golden with a few light-brown spots on the edges, careful not to overcook or burn.

10. Sprinkle with salt and serve fresh out of the oven when the onions are still soft.

VARIATIONS

HERBED ONION RINGS

Add 2 teaspoons Italian seasoning.

TEXAN ONION RINGS

Add 1 teaspoon cayenne powder, more or less to taste.

"OVEN-DEHYDRATED" KALE CHIPS

MAKES 2–3 SERVINGS

RECIPE BY DREENA BURTON

The best kale chips are made with a dehydrator, since it slowly dries the leaves, as opposed to an oven, which can cook the leaves and make them taste burned and bitter. After spending far too much money on store-bought kale chips, I decided to create this unique recipe. Here, you use your oven to mimic "dehydrating" by alternating a very low temperature with turning your oven off. The chips slowly dry and become crunchy and tasty without getting browned or burned.

1 bunch fresh kale (curly or dinosaur/
   black kale)
2 teaspoons tahini
2 teaspoons fresh lemon juice
1 teaspoon tamari (or coconut aminos for soy-
   free option)

½ teaspoon maple syrup
2½–3 tablespoons nutritional yeast
⅛ teaspoon sea salt

1. Fully wash kale leaves by submerging bunch of kale in a sink of cold water. Agitate to release any debris.

2. Strip the leaves from the stems and place leaves in a salad spinner. Spin several times to remove as much water as possible. If leaves are still a little damp, use a kitchen towel to blot and dry kale leaves.

3. Turn oven to lowest setting possible. For most ovens, this is 170°F. Get two large baking sheets ready by lining with parchment paper.

4. In a large bowl, combine the tahini, lemon juice, tamari or coconut aminos, and maple syrup.

5. Stir or whisk through until fully smooth in the bottom of the bowl.

6. Add kale leaves and toss through with your hands, gently incorporating all of the tahini sauce and massaging it through all the leaves.

7. Add the nutritional yeast and continue to work through the kale leaves.

8. Transfer the kale to your prepared baking sheets, spreading them out to give the leaves space to dry. Sprinkle the leaves with salt.

9. Place baking sheets in oven on two racks. Bake at 170°F for an hour.

10. After an hour, turn off oven, rotate trays, and then let the trays sit in the oven for another 30 minutes.

11. After this time, turn oven on again at 170°F and let bake for another 15–20 minutes.

12. Check kale; if it is completely dry and crispy, remove from oven. If not, turn off heat and let sit in the warm oven for another 30–40 minutes (or longer). By then, the kale should be crispy and also still fairly vibrant green!

TIPS

If your oven can go lower than 170°F, the process may take another 20–30 minutes.

If you like heat, add a few pinches of chili powder or other seasonings as you like. Stick with dry seasonings and also remember that the flavor intensifies once the leaves are dried, so go easy to start!

To re-crisp leftovers, just reheat at same low temperature until the chips return to a flaky, crispy texture.

BAKED TORTILLA CHIPS

YIELD AMOUNT VARIES

RECIPE BY CHEF AJ

Make sure you get tortillas that are made only of corn or just corn and lime.

Corn tortillas
Herbs or sodium-free seasonings (optional)

1. Preheat oven to 375°F.
2. Cut each tortilla into fourths.
3. Place tortilla pieces on a cookie sheet covered with parchment paper or a silicone baking mat and lightly spray each chip with water.
4. Sprinkle with herbs or sodium-free seasonings, if desired.
5. Bake for 10 minutes. Turn chips over and lightly spray again with water.
6. Bake for another 8–10 minutes until crisp.

NACHO "CHEESE" SAUCE

MAKES 4 CUPS 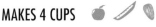 RECIPE BY CHEF AJ

2 cups water
1 can cannellini beans, drained and rinsed, or
   1½ cups cooked beans
1 roasted red bell pepper
⅓ cup raw cashews
4 tablespoons nutritional yeast

3 tablespoons fresh lemon juice
2 teaspoons smoked paprika
½ teaspoon garlic powder
½ teaspoon onion powder
½ teaspoon chipotle powder
3 tablespoons arrowroot powder

1. In a blender, blend all ingredients, except for the arrowroot, until smooth.

2. Leaving about ½ cup of the contents in the blender, pour mixture into a medium saucepan and heat over medium heat.

3. Add the arrowroot powder to the blender and blend again.

4. Slowly add remaining mixture to the saucepan, stirring constantly until thickened.

TIPS

This is delicious as a topping for nachos made with baked tortilla chips. It is also delicious as a sauce for pasta, broccoli, and potatoes.

Once refrigerated, you can use it as a "cheese" spread.

DESSERTS

DARK CHOCOLATE, SWEET POTATO &
BLACK BEAN BROWNIES | 256

CHOCOLATE DATE-NUT LOLLIPOPS

MAKES 8–10 LOLLIPOPS   RECIPE BY LAURA THEODORE

Fun, fun, fun! That's how I describe these lovely little lollipops. The dates help to hold the pops together while also standing in for much of the processed sugar. They're perfect for any party, whether you are entertaining kids or adults!

FOR THE LOLLIPOPS
½ cup vegan dark chocolate chips (grain-sweetened variety works well)
6 large Medjool dates, pitted
¼ cup whole pecans
⅛ teaspoon vanilla extract

FOR THE TOPPINGS
2 tablespoons ground pecans, walnuts, or hazelnuts (optional)
2 tablespoons dark, nondairy cocoa powder (optional)

1. Put the vegan chocolate chips in a double boiler (see Tip) over medium-low heat. When the chocolate has melted, remove from the heat.

2. Meanwhile, put the dates, pecans, and vanilla in a high-performance blending appliance and process to the consistency of soft dough.

3. Transfer the date mixture to a medium bowl, pour in the melted chocolate, and stir until well combined.

4. Put the date mixture in the freezer for 7–15 minutes or until the chocolate has set enough to roll into small balls.

5. Line a small baking sheet with unbleached parchment paper.

6. Spoon out a heaping tablespoon of the chocolate mixture and quickly roll it into a ball. Roll it in one of the optional toppings until completely coated. Place it on the prepared baking sheet.

7. Continue in this way, forming all of the remaining chocolate mixture into balls and coating them in one of the optional coatings.

8. Insert the end of a lollipop stick into each chocolate ball and place all lollipops upright in two separate mugs or shallow glasses, making sure they do not touch each other.

9. Refrigerate for 1–2 hours before serving. For a festive presentation, wrap each lollipop in cellophane and tie with a pretty ribbon.

10. Stored in an airtight container in the refrigerator, leftover lollipops will keep for up to 3 days.

TIP

If you don't have a double boiler, you can improvise one with a heatproof bowl and a saucepan. The bowl should partially (not completely) fit into the saucepan. Fill the saucepan with enough water so that when the bowl rests in the saucepan, the water doesn't touch the bottom of the bowl. Bring the water to a simmer. Put the ingredients in the bowl and place the bowl in the saucepan.

COCONUT PILLOWS

MAKES 13–15 COOKIES

RECIPE BY DREENA BURTON

These yummy, nibbly cookies are made nutritious with oat flour, nut butter, and sweetened with maple syrup, orange juice, and a touch of coconut sugar.

1¼ cups oat flour (use certified gluten-free for that option)
½ cup unsweetened shredded coconut
2 tablespoons coconut sugar (can substitute another unrefined sugar)
1 teaspoon baking powder
¼ teaspoon baking soda
⅛ teaspoon sea salt

Few pinches of ground cinnamon (optional)
¼ cup nut butter (unsalted; I prefer raw almond butter or cashew, see Tips)
¼ cup maple syrup
2 tablespoons fresh orange juice
½–1 teaspoon orange zest (optional, zest orange before juicing)
1½ teaspoons vanilla extract

1. Preheat oven to 350°F.
2. In a bowl, combine the oat flour, coconut, coconut sugar, baking powder, baking soda, salt, and cinnamon.
3. In a small bowl, first combine the nut butter with the maple syrup, whisking to smooth out.
4. Add in the orange juice, zest, and vanilla and stir through.
5. Add wet mixture to dry and stir until just combined (do not overmix).
6. Place batter in fridge to chill for about 20–30 minutes.
7. After chilling, use a small cookie scoop to place rounds of the dough (about a tablespoon or rounded tablespoon in size) on a baking sheet lined with parchment paper. The batter will be sticky, so rinse the scoop a few times through if you like.
8. Bake cookies for 10 minutes, then remove and let cool on the sheet for 1–2 minutes. Transfer to a cookie sheet.

Depending on the nut butter used, the batter can be thicker or looser. Start with 1¼ cups oat flour and if the batter is a little loose after stirring, sprinkle in an extra tablespoon of flour. Note that the batter will also firm up with chilling.

Other nut butters can be substituted, though almond and cashew are my favorites. If using a seed butter, the batter will need extra sweetness, so adjust with a few teaspoons of maple syrup to taste and a touch more cinnamon.

CLAFOUTI

MAKES 8 SERVINGS

RECIPE BY CHEF AJ

1 pound strawberries
1 pound ripe bananas (about 3 bananas)
10 ounces sweetened fruit jam
2 cups gluten-free oats

1 teaspoon baking powder
½ cup unsweetened applesauce
1 cup unsweetened apple juice

1. Preheat oven to 350°F.

2. Slice fruit and mix well with jam. Place in an 8 × 8 silicone pan.

3. Place oats in a blender and blend into a flour, then pour oat flour into a bowl. Mix in remaining ingredients and place evenly over fruit.

4. Bake for 45–50 minutes until golden brown.

5. Serve warm with Pear Crème Anglais (p. 247).

PEAR CRÈME ANGLAIS

MAKES 1½ CUPS

RECIPE BY CHEF AJ

1 28-ounce jar pears in their own juice (see Tip)

⅓ cup raw cashews (optional)

1 tablespoon vanilla extract

1 teaspoon xanthan gum (optional)

1. Drain pears, reserving juice for another use.

2. In a blender, blend pears until smooth.

3. Add remaining ingredients and blend until incorporated. Chill.

4. Serve over warm Clafouti (p. 246).

TIP

You can use fresh pears, but you need to peel them first and they must be ripe and soft.

DREAMY BAKED BANANAS

MAKES 2–3 SERVINGS   RECIPE BY DREENA BURTON

It seems silly that something so basic, so "real," and so effortless can taste so impossibly dreamy. But dessert food dreams do come true, and this one is especially memorable in the morning if paired with a nondairy ice cream.

2 tablespoons macadamia nut butter (or raw cashew or raw almond butter)
¼ cup nondairy milk
2 teaspoons fresh lemon juice
½ teaspoon vanilla extract
¼ teaspoon ground cinnamon
⅛ teaspoon freshly grated nutmeg (optional)

⅛ teaspoon sea salt
3 ripe bananas (but not overripe)
2 tablespoons raisins or chopped dates (optional, can substitute or add chopped nuts)
1–2 tablespoons coconut sugar for sprinkling (optional)

1. Preheat oven to 400°F.

2. In a bowl, whisk together the nut butter, milk, lemon juice, vanilla, cinnamon, nutmeg, and salt. It will be thick but should be smooth.

3. Transfer to a baking dish or glass pie plate.

4. Peel the bananas and slice in half lengthwise.

5. Place banana slices in the mixture, then gently flip so both sides are coated.

6. Sprinkle on the raisins or chopped dates, followed by the coconut sugar, if using.

7. Bake for 17–20 minutes. Serve hot or warm preferably. While still good cooled, this dessert is definitely best a little warm—ice cream prefers it that way!

> **TIP**
>
> When I make this recipe, our girls polish off the entire dish in a blink. So I'd say it *can* serve three, but more likely two . . . or maybe that's just in my house!

STRAWBERRY BABYCAKES

MAKES 9 BABYCAKES

RECIPE BY CHRISTINA ROSS

These babies are fuss-free since you don't have to worry about temperature or timing with these little cuties. Simply pull out your food processor and ice cream scoop and moments later you'll be biting right into one of these bursting beauties. Superb to serve any time of day!

1 cup strawberries
2 tablespoons fresh lemon juice
⅛ cup and 2 teaspoons grade A light amber maple syrup, divided
½ tablespoon chia seeds

1 cup cashews
¼ cup almonds
½ teaspoon vanilla bean
2 teaspoons almond extract

1. Using a paring knife, remove the stem and the white center from the strawberries. Press your thumb into the center of each strawberry to gently spread it open and flatten it.

2. In a small mixing bowl, add the strawberries, lemon juice, 2 teaspoons maple syrup, and chia seeds. Stir gently and let sit while making the cakes.

3. Using a food processor, process the cashews and almonds into a fine flour. Add in the vanilla bean, almond extract, and ⅛ cup maple syrup and process until mixture holds together (test this by pinching it between your fingers).

4. Using an ice cream scoop, scoop the mixture into a ball and set onto a plate or piece of parchment paper. Once you have all of the "batter" scooped, press your thumb gently in the center of each ball to make an impression about ¼-inch deep but not all the way through.

5. Fill the center of each ball with the strawberry filling.

6. Eat right away or store covered in the fridge.

PUMPKIN CHIA PUDDING

MAKES 3–4 SERVINGS   RECIPE BY DREENA BURTON

If you love pumpkin flavors in baking, you'll love this "instant" pumpkin pudding! The chia seeds are the magical ingredient to thicken the pudding, and when pureed they are not visible for any little palates that might be, ahem, picky!

¾ cup pure pumpkin (see Tips)
¾ cup unsweetened plain or vanilla nondairy milk (see Tips)
¼ cup maple syrup
1–2 tablespoons coconut sugar (or pinch of stevia, see Tips)
3 tablespoons white chia seeds (black will discolor pudding some)
1 teaspoon ground cinnamon
¼ teaspoon freshly grated nutmeg

⅛ teaspoon ground allspice
Pinch of ground ginger (optional, I omit it when making for the kiddos)
⅛ teaspoon sea salt (slightly rounded)
½ teaspoon vanilla extract (or vanilla seeds from 1 bean)
Dark chocolate shavings, coconut whipped cream, vegan cookie crumbles for topping (optional)

1. In a blender, add all ingredients. Blend for a minute or more (depending on blender) until the seeds are fully pulverized and the pudding begins to thicken (it will thicken more as it refrigerates).

2. Taste, and if you'd like it sweeter, add 1–2 teaspoons more coconut sugar or maple syrup (not too much maple syrup or it will become loose).

3. Transfer mixture to a large bowl or to 3–4 individual serving bowls (e.g., ramekins), and refrigerate until chilled, about 30 minutes or more (it will thicken more with chilling, but really can be eaten straight away).

4. Serve, sprinkling with optional toppings, if desired.

TIPS

Canned pumpkin can really vary in consistency. Some are thinner; others a little more loose. I use Farmer's Market brand, which is very thick and dense and, as a bonus, organic.

If using sweetened vanilla milk, reduce the sweetener to taste.

I love coconut sugar and I think it adds a buttery-sweet note to recipes. You may not need or want it in this pudding, however; the maple syrup may add enough sweetness for your taste (and the type of milk used will also affect sweetness). If you'd rather use stevia, add just 1–2 pinches and test along the way, since too much stevia can ruin the flavor. You can also add a little extra maple syrup, but no more than about 1–2 tablespoons, since the pudding can become a little loose.

RASPBERRY GANACHE FUDGE CAKE

MAKES ABOUT 6 SERVINGS   RECIPE BY ANI PHYO

I use carob in my cake to cut down on the caffeine, and because I love carob for its malty rich flavor. This cake is one of my favorites.

FOR THE FUDGE CAKE
3 cups dry walnuts
⅔ cup unsweetened cacao powder or carob powder
¼ teaspoon sea salt
1 cup pitted Medjool dates

FOR THE FROSTING
⅓ cup semi-soft pitted Medjool dates
¼ cup agave syrup
½ cup ripe avocado flesh (from about 1 medium avocado)
⅓ cup cacao powder

FOR THE FILLING
½ cup raspberries

1. Combine the walnuts, cacao powder, and salt in the food processor and pulse until coarsely mixed. Avoid overprocessing.
2. Add the dates and pulse until mixed well. Shape into two stackable cakes of desired shape and set aside.
3. Combine the dates and agave syrup in the food processor and process until smooth.
4. Add the avocado and process until smooth.
5. Add the cacao powder and process until smooth.
6. To serve, frost the top of one of the cakes with half the frosting and top with the raspberries.
7. Stack the second cake on top and frost the top and side. Serve immediately or place in the refrigerator for a couple hours to firm up.
8. The cake on its own will keep in the fridge for many weeks. The frosting will keep separately in the fridge for 1 week. The assembled cake with raspberries will keep in the fridge for up to 3 days.

DARK CHOCOLATE, SWEET POTATO & BLACK BEAN BROWNIES SEE PICTURE ON PAGE 241

MAKES 16+ BROWNIES RECIPE BY HEATHER CROSBY

I do love to sneak unexpected, nutrient-rich ingredients into treats, and this gluten-free recipe is a perfect example. Who knew black beans, sweet potato, and dark chocolate could combine into such fudge-like decadence?

FOR THE WET INGREDIENTS
1 cup dry black beans (soaked/cooked yields 2¼ cups)
⅔ cup sweet potato, diced
2 teaspoons vanilla extract
1 3-ounce bar of gluten-free, nondairy dark chocolate
⅓ cup grade B maple syrup
¾ cup water

FOR THE DRY INGREDIENTS
1½ cups almond flour
⅓ cup Sucanat
½ cup raw cacao powder or cocoa powder
1 teaspoon baking powder
½ teaspoon fine ground sea salt

1. Soak dry beans for 8–12 hours.

2. Rinse beans well and transfer to a pot. Fill pot with enough water to cover beans 3 inches (about 6 cups). Bring beans to a boil, uncovered, and then reduce heat to medium. Cover and let beans simmer for 45–60 minutes until cooked. Check water level every 20 minutes or so, adding more water as necessary.

3. While beans cook, wash, peel, dice, and steam sweet potatoes for 10–15 minutes until easily pierced with a fork. Set aside.

4. Preheat oven to 350°F and line baking dish with parchment paper.

5. Once beans are cooked (and drained if necessary) and potatoes are steamed, place all wet ingredients into the food processor and pulse until very smooth.

6. Sift or stir together dry ingredients.

7. Fold together wet and dry ingredients and transfer to parchment-lined baking dish.

8. Bake for 60 minutes. Remove from oven and allow to cool in baking dish before serving.

You can use canned beans for this recipe, but I recommend starting with dry beans to reduce aluminum intake, to boost flavor, and for optimal digestion and assimilation of nutritional benefits.

If you don't have a steamer, you can roast diced sweet potato in a glass baking dish at 350°F for 20 minutes or until easily pierced with a fork. Add 2 tablespoons water to the bottom of your dish—it will help soften the potatoes as they roast.

Line your baking dish with one strip of parchment running horizontally and one running vertically, with about 1 inch of parchment up over sides. Parchment paper makes it easy to remove and slice brownies once baked. Just lift out the parchment-wrapped brownies and slice.

For a triple dark chocolate brownie, top batter with shaved chocolate before baking.

Store in an airtight glass container in the fridge for up to two weeks. You can also freeze brownies in an airtight container and simply thaw when you want a treat.

PEANUT BUTTER AND JELLY COOKIES

MAKES 18 COOKIES   RECIPE BY LAURA THEODORE

Like peanut butter and jelly sandwiches packed into sweet cookie confections, these gems truly shine. With a delectable jelly center and crisp base, they make the perfect afternoon snack paired with a tall glass of nondairy milk.

1 cup whole-wheat flour
½ teaspoon baking powder
⅛ teaspoon sea salt
⅓ cup creamy peanut butter
⅓ cup maple syrup

3 tablespoons nondairy milk
1 teaspoon vanilla extract
½–⅔ cup raspberry, strawberry, or blueberry
   preserves, jelly, or jam

1. Preheat oven to 375°F. Line a large baking sheet with unbleached parchment paper.

2. Put the flour, baking powder, and salt in a medium bowl and stir with a dry whisk to combine.

3. Add the peanut butter, maple syrup, nondairy milk, and vanilla to the flour mixture and stir vigorously until smooth and well combined. The dough will be stiff.

4. For each cookie, drop about 1 tablespoon of the dough onto the prepared baking sheet, using a cookie scoop or rounded spoon.

5. With your thumb, press down gently into the middle of each cookie, making a small well. Fill each well with 1 teaspoon of the preserves.

6. Bake for 16–18 minutes, or until the cookies are golden brown around the edges. Put the baking sheet on a wire rack.

7. Let the cookies cool on the baking sheet for 15 minutes before transferring to a serving platter to further cool.

8. Stored in an airtight container in the refrigerator, the cookies will keep for about 3 days.

MINT CHOCOLATE MOUSSE TORTE

MAKES 12–16 SLICES   RECIPE BY CHEF AJ

FOR THE FILLING

1 pound pitted dates soaked in 16 ounces
    unsweetened chocolate almond milk
1 tablespoon vanilla extract
1–2 teaspoons peppermint extract, more or
    less to taste
½ cup raw cacao powder
3 cups walnuts
½ cup unsweetened coconut

FOR THE CRUST

2 cups raw walnuts
¼ cup raw cacao powder
2 cups pitted dates
1 tablespoon vanilla extract
1 teaspoon peppermint extract
½ cup raw cacao nibs

1. To make the filling in a food processor, process soaked dates and extracts until very smooth.

2. Add ½ cup cacao powder and process again until smooth. Place this in a bowl.

3. Process the nuts into a nut butter–like consistency.

4. Add coconut and process again. Add this to the date mixture and stir well by hand until all of the ingredients are completely incorporated. Set aside.

5. To make the crust in a food processor, process 2 cups nuts into a powder. Do not overprocess or you will have a nut butter.

6. Add ¼ cup cacao powder, then add 2 cups pitted dates, a few at a time, until the mixture clumps together. Stop the machine and if you can easily roll a ball from the mixture and it sticks together, you don't need to add any more dates.

7. Add extracts and process again briefly. Press the crust into a springform pan.

8. Spread filling over the top and freeze until solid.

9. Garnish with raw cacao nibs.

PEANUT BUTTER FUDGE TRUFFLES

MAKES ABOUT 3 DOZEN TRUFFLES

FOR THE DATE PASTE
1 pound pitted dates
1 cup liquid (water, unsweetened nondairy milk, or unsweetened juice)

FOR THE CHOCOLATE FUNDUE
1 cup date paste
1 cup peanut butter (no salt or sugar)
½ cup raw cacao powder
½ cup unsweetened nondairy milk
1 tablespoon vanilla extract
Crushed peanuts

1. Soak dates in liquid overnight or for several hours until much of the liquid is absorbed.

2. In a food processor, process dates and liquid until completely smooth. You can store date paste in the refrigerator.

3. Place all ingredients for Chocolate FUNdue in a food processor and process until ingredients are incorporated, scraping down sides if necessary. Chill FUNdue until firm.

4. Using a small retractable cookie scoop, drop FUNdue into crushed peanuts and coat evenly.

THE CHINA STUDY ALL-STAR COLLECTION

PEANUT BUTTER MOUSSE TARTLETS

MAKES 12 TARTLETS   RECIPE BY LAURA THEODORE

Peanut butter has never been yummier than when it is piped into these pretty little fruit-and-seed mini-crusts. These creamy, chewy, and crusty gems are the ideal choice to round out any elegant meal.

12 large Medjool dates, pitted and chopped
½ cup unsalted, raw sunflower seeds
⅔ cup cubed firm regular tofu (sprouted variety is preferred)

4 tablespoons creamy peanut butter
4 tablespoons maple syrup
12 vegan chocolate chips

1. Put the dates and sunflower seeds in a food processor and process to a smooth dough.

2. Put the date mixture in a medium bowl and pull it together to form a ball.

3. Divide the date mixture into 12 parts and roll each into a ball.

4. Press each ball into the shape of a cup, one at a time, using the cups in a mini-muffin baking tin as a guide.

5. Using an offset spatula or table knife, carefully remove the date cups from the mini-muffin molds, and place them on a flat tray or plate that has been lined with parchment paper.

6. Put the tofu, peanut butter, and maple syrup in a blender and process until very smooth.

7. Spoon the mixture into a pastry bag fitted with a large star pastry tip (see Tip).

8. Pipe the filling into each of the date cups and top each with a single vegan chocolate chip.

9. Cover and refrigerate for 5–6 hours before serving.

TIP

If you do not have a pastry bag, simply spoon the filling into the cups.

PEPPERMINT CHOCOLATE CHUNK ICE CREAM

MAKES 4–6 SERVINGS   RECIPE BY HEATHER CROSBY

A simple and refreshing recipe that can be prepared with or without an ice cream maker.

2 14-ounce cans coconut milk
¼ cup maple syrup
2 teaspoons peppermint extract
1½ teaspoons vanilla extract
10 peppermint leaves (optional)

Pinch of fine ground sea salt
1 3-ounce gluten-free, nondairy chocolate bar, roughly chopped, or ½–1 cup gluten-free, nondairy chocolate chips

1. Blend together all ingredients except chocolate bar.

2. If using an ice cream maker, chill ice cream mixture in the refrigerator until cold, then process in the ice cream maker according to the manufacturer's instructions. Once firm, fold in chocolate bar and freeze until ready to serve.

3. If not using an ice cream maker, fold chocolate bar into ice cream mixture and freeze until ready to serve.

TIPS

I often like to prepare this recipe with leaves from a chocolate mint plant. The best place to find chocolate mint? Grow your own!

Make your ice cream green by adding ½–1 teaspoon of liquid chlorophyll—a detoxifying natural "dye."

Be sure to plan accordingly and thaw your ice cream on the counter for 10–15 minutes before serving.

EASY BREEZY SUNDAY COBBLER

MAKES 8 SERVINGS   RECIPE BY CHRISTINA ROSS

You don't have to wait until Sunday to make this super simple and satisfying dessert. I love the ease, simplicity, and versatility of this recipe as you can change up the ingredients to come up with your family's favorite combinations. Have fun experimenting with this unintimidating no-bake cobbler.

3 fresh peaches
3 fresh plums
1 cup pecans

½ cup coconut flour
2 tablespoons and 1 teaspoon coconut nectar, divided

1. Chop the peaches and plums into bite-size cubes.
2. Spread the chopped fruit into a 9-inch glass pie dish or casserole dish.
3. Add the pecans, coconut flour, and 2 tablespoons coconut nectar to a food processor and process until the mixture is crumbly and gently sticks together.
4. Pour the crumble mixture over the fruit covering the entire dish.
5. Drizzle the remaining nectar over the top.
6. You can chill this cobbler, warm it up, or serve it as I do—immediately.

THE CHINA STUDY ALL-STAR COLLECTION

SPICED BLUEBERRY COBBLER

MAKES 4–6 SERVINGS

RECIPE BY ANI PHYO

The sweetness of blueberries with a hint of chai spices means big flavor in this easy cobbler. Blueberries have powerful antioxidants and are packed with vitamins A, B, and C to help prevent skin damage caused by stress and the sun. Fresh blueberries are one of the many fruits I enjoy picking in the summertime. They're delicious straight off the vine and in this crunchy cobbler.

FOR THE CRUST
1 cup dry almonds
1 teaspoon ground nutmeg
1 teaspoon ground cinnamon
½ teaspoon salt
1 cup pitted semi-soft Medjool dates

FOR THE FILLING
4 cups blueberries
¼ cup agave syrup (optional)

1. Combine the almonds, nutmeg, cinnamon, and salt in the food processor and pulse into coarse pieces.
2. Add the dates and process until mixed well. Sprinkle half of the crust into the bottom of a loaf pan.
3. Combine the blueberries and agave syrup, if using, in a mixing bowl and toss to mix well.
4. Scoop into the loaf pan. Top with the remaining crust, press gently, and serve.
5. Will keep for 2–3 days in the fridge. The crust will keep for several weeks when stored on its own in the fridge.

> **TIP**
>
> Serve the cobbler parfait-style in a glass: Start with about ½ cup cobbler in the bottom of the glass. Add a scoop of your favorite nondairy ice cream and top with another ¼–½ cup cobbler.

BLUEBERRY DREAMSICLES

MAKES 6 DREAMSICLES   RECIPE BY CHRISTINA ROSS

This is a recipe the whole family is guaranteed to love. What's even better is that you can serve these for breakfast or as a snack. The dreamsicles are fun and simple to make; as you blend the mixture, have the little ones pick twigs from the yard to use in the molds.

⅛ cup grade A light amber maple syrup
1 lemon, juiced
1 cup blueberries

1 15-ounce can whole coconut milk, chilled
for 24 hours

1. In a small mixing bowl, pour maple syrup and lemon juice over blueberries and mix gently.

2. Put coconut milk in a mixer and whip until thickened, adding in the blueberries while whipping. Some of the berries will break down, releasing their juices and creating texture. If you want the berries whole, hand mix them in gently using a rubber spatula.

3. Pour mixture into popsicle molds. Place a 6-inch twig in place of the stem for each. Freeze for 2 hours.

4. Run the mold under warm water for a few seconds and gently pull dreamsicles from mold.

ITALIAN ICES WITH LEMON SYRUP AND TUTTI FRUTTI SAUCE

MAKES 4 SERVINGS   RECIPE BY ANI PHYO

It takes only a few minutes to make this dessert of refreshing ice, tart lemon syrup, and a beautiful berry sauce. It's delicious and full of antioxidants and vitamin C to keep our summer skin looking youthful.

FOR THE LEMON SYRUP
4 lemons, zested and juiced
¼ cup agave syrup

FOR THE TUTTI FRUTTI SAUCE
1 cup strawberries
¼ cup agave syrup
1 tablespoon vanilla extract or the seeds from 1 vanilla bean
½ cup blackberries
½ cup raspberries
4 cups ice

1. To make the lemon syrup, combine the lemon juice, zest, and agave syrup in a mixing bowl and mix well.

2. To make the tutti frutti sauce, combine the strawberries, agave syrup, and vanilla in a blender. Gently pulse to a chunky texture. Spoon into a bowl and stir in the blackberries and raspberries.

3. Place the ice in the food processor and chop into tiny pieces.

4. Use an ice cream scooper to tightly pack and scoop the ice into 4 dishes. Top with lemon syrup first, then the tutti frutti sauce. Enjoy immediately.

LEMON-BERRY SORBET

MAKES 6–8 SERVINGS   RECIPE BY DEL SROUFE

If you can find fresh, in-season berries at the farmers' market, buy a lot of them, then freeze what you don't eat and have them handy for tasty treats like this one.

1 quart frozen berries
1 ripe banana, sliced and frozen (optional)
½ tablespoon stevia extract, more or less to taste

¼ cup fresh lemon juice
½ teaspoon lemon zest
2 tablespoons vodka (optional)

1. Place the berries and banana slices, if using, in a food processor and pulse until they are the size of peas.

2. Add the stevia extract, lemon juice and zest, and vodka, if using, and puree until smooth.

3. Place the mixture into a shallow dish and freeze for 2–3 hours, stirring every 30 minutes or so until firm.

> **TIP**
>
> I add a banana and a little vodka to this recipe to make the sorbet less icy, but you can leave both out if you prefer. You can also make this dish in your ice cream maker for a smoother texture.

MANGO SORBET

MAKES 4 SERVINGS   RECIPE BY ANI PHYO

This recipe calls for frozen mangoes, my favorite fruit. I always prefer fresh everything, so I'll prepare fresh mango a day or two before and then freeze it. Frozen mango from the freezer aisle will work, too.

2 cups chopped frozen mangoes
1 cup water
⅓ cup agave syrup

1. Combine the mangoes, water, and agave syrup in a high-speed blender and blend until smooth. Serve immediately. Or for an icier, more solid texture, scoop into a container and place in freezer for an hour or more.

2. To make in an ice cream maker: Chill the mixture in the freezer for an hour or so, then scoop into the ice cream maker and follow the manufacturer's instructions.

3. Will keep for several weeks in freezer. Let thaw for 10 minutes before serving.

PAPAYA MILKSHAKES

MAKES 4 CUPS   RECIPE BY LEANNE CAMPBELL

3 cups chopped fresh papaya

1 cup unsweetened almond milk

1 teaspoon vanilla extract

1 teaspoon ground cinnamon

1½ cups ice

¼ cup agave nectar

1. Place all ingredients in a blender.

2. Blend on high speed, stopping occasionally to move any fruit or ice toward the blades. Serve immediately.

CRANBERRY-APPLE CRISP

MAKES 8 SERVINGS

RECIPE BY CHEF AJ

This dish is delicious served cold the next day with a hot cup of tea.

4 large apples (I prefer Gala or Braeburn)
2 cups 5-Minute Cranberry Relish (p. 214)
2 cups gluten-free oats
1 cup unsweetened apple juice

2 teaspoons ground cinnamon
½ teaspoon ground nutmeg
1 tablespoon vanilla extract

1. Preheat oven to 350°F.
2. Peel, core, and thinly slice apples.
3. Mix with 2 cups cranberry relish and pour into an 8 × 8 silicone baking pan.
4. In a separate bowl, mix oats with apple juice, spices, and vanilla. Stir until well mixed.
5. Evenly place on top of the apple-cranberry mixture.
6. Bake for 50–60 minutes until topping is golden brown.

APPENDIX

MEASUREMENT GUIDE

ABBREVIATION KEY

tsp   =   teaspoon

tbsp   =   tablespoon

dsp   =   dessert spoon

U.S. STANDARD—U.K.

¼ tsp   =   ¼ tsp (scant)

½ tsp   =   ½ tsp (scant)

¾ tsp   =   ½ tsp (rounded)

1 tsp   =   ¾ tsp (slightly rounded)

1 tbsp   =   2½ tsp

¼ cup   =   ¼ cup minus 1 dsp

⅓ cup   =   ¼ cup plus 1 tsp

½ cup   =   ⅓ cup plus 2 dsp

⅔ cup   =   ½ cup plus 1 tbsp

¾ cup   =   ½ cup plus 2 tbsp

1 cup   =   ¾ cup plus 2 dsp

DIETARY SYMBOLS

Through the use of the following symbols, each recipe in this cookbook shows which parts of the plant the dish incorporates. It's important to consume a variety of the categories each day in order to obtain all the nutrients you need.

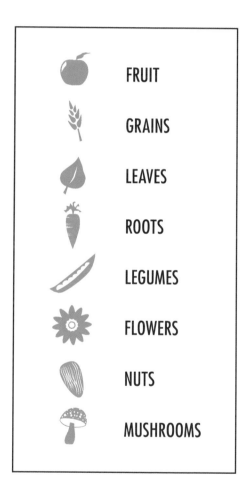

FRUIT

GRAINS

LEAVES

ROOTS

LEGUMES

FLOWERS

NUTS

MUSHROOMS

NUTRITIONAL VALUE

NUTRITIONAL VALUE

Here's a look at some of the nutritional value of the eight categories (seven types of plant parts plus mushrooms):

FRUITS are packed with vitamin C and other phytochemicals.

GRAINS abound in carbohydrates, fiber, minerals, and B vitamins.

LEAVES are lush with antioxidant vitamins, fiber, and complex carbohydrates.

ROOTS have lots of carbohydrates; some have carotenoids.

LEGUMES are a hearty source of protein, fiber, and iron.

FLOWERS are rich in antioxidants and phytochemicals.

NUTS are loaded with omega-3 fats, vitamin E, and protein.

MUSHROOMS offer a good supply of selenium and other antioxidants.

To be consistent with the message in *The China Study* and especially its sequel, *Whole*, nutrient compositions are not presented with the recipes. Nutrient contents in different samples of the same food often are highly variable, leading consumers to be concerned with trivial and meaningless differences instead of the far more important health characteristics of food variety and wholesomeness.

INDEX

ABOUT THE CONTRIBUTORS

CHEF AJ

Chef AJ has followed a plant-based diet for over thirty-six years. She is a chef, culinary instructor, professional speaker, and author. With her comedy background, she has made appearances on *The Tonight Show with Johnny Carson*, *The Tonight Show with Jay Leno*, *David Letterman*, and more.

In Los Angeles, Chef AJ teaches her popular Intro Class, which includes cooking instruction, nutritional advice, song parodies, and flat-out fun. She discusses food addiction and addresses the emotional side of eating. Never content to leave her audience with mere "just do it" advice, she teaches:

- how to create meals to transform your health
- how to deal with cravings
- how to deal with food addiction

Chef AJ is the author of the popular book *Unprocessed: How to Achieve Vibrant Health and Your Ideal Weight*. The book is part confessional memoir, part delectable recipes. It chronicles her journey from being a junk-food vegan faced with a diagnosis of pre-cancerous polyps to learning how to create foods that heal the body. Many of her recipes can be seen on her YouTube cooking show, *The Chef and the Dietitian*.

She holds a Certificate in Plant-Based Nutrition from Cornell University and is a member of the American College of Lifestyle Medicine.

UNPROCESSED: HOW TO ACHIEVE VIBRANT HEALTH AND YOUR IDEAL WEIGHT
(Hail to the Kale Publishing, 2011)

ANI PHYO

Ani Phyo is a renowned raw food chef and show host, health coach, nutritionist, and the author of five books, including *Ani's Raw Food Kitchen*, *Ani's Raw Food Essentials*, and *Ani's Raw Food Detox*. She lives in Los Angeles. AniPhyo.com; @AniPhyo

ANI'S RAW FOOD KITCHEN
(Da Capo Press, 2007)

ANI'S RAW FOOD DESSERTS
(Da Capo Press, 2009)

ANI'S RAW FOOD ASIA
(Da Capo Press, 2011)

ANI'S RAW FOOD ESSENTIALS
(Da Capo Press, 2012)

CHRISTINA ROSS

Christina Ross is an Ambassador of Healthy Living, dynamic conscious chef, educator, food writer, and blogger. She is the founder of PatisseRaw, a transitional raw and vegan dessert line sold online and locally in Southern California. PatisseRaw has attracted a health-conscious celebrity following and has also been featured on NBC's *Today Show*.

Christina's recipes and healthful lifestyle tips have been published in *Natural Child World* magazine through her column "Love-Fed." Christina also contributes recipes and articles to popular sites such as Raw Food Recipes, Clean Food Living, Vegan Food Share, Organic Soul, She Knows, Just Eat Real Food, RawGuru, and Kris Carr's My Crazy Sexy Life Community.

Through Christina's ongoing partnership with local Whole Foods Markets she delivers her recipes to audiences of all ages. She's been brought into schools to prepare her recipes for over 500 kids and to teach children how to prepare healthful, simple, and delicious meals.

Additionally, Christina keeps her many fans full of nutrient-rich content through her blog Love-Fed.com and through television appearances, which have taken her to Chicago's *Good Day Chicago* on Fox 32 as well as San Diego for another episode on *San Diego Living CW6*. She's currently working on her first cookbook to be published by BenBella Books.

Christina's contribution to happy and healthy living can be found all over the web at the following social media links:

BLOG:
love-fed.com
COMPANY:
patisseraw.com
FACEBOOK:
facebook.com/lovefedrecipes
YOUTUBE:
youtube.com/user/LoveFedChristina

PINTEREST:
pinterest.com/lovefedrecipes
TWITTER:
twitter.com/Lovefedrecipes
INSTAGRAM:
instagram.com/lovefed

LOVE-FED
available
February
2015

CHRISTY MORGAN

Christy Morgan, known as The Blissful Chef, has been tantalizing taste buds for years as a vegan chef, cooking instructor, food writer, and cookbook author. Christy's mission is to show that a whole food, plant-based diet can be delicious and easy and will bring more energy and bliss into your life! Now living in Austin, Texas, she offers cooking classes and health programs for corporations and families who want to get their health on track. You'll find her recipe contributions in the *Skinny Bitch: Ultimate Everyday Cookbook* by Kim Barnouin and articles written for various platforms across the web. Her first cookbook, *Blissful Bites: Plant-based Meals That Nourish Mind, Body, and Planet*, is available in bookstores. Her new online wellness program, Wellness Reboot, gives you a chance to work with Christy from anywhere in the world to transform your life and reboot your health.

Christy has contributed to VegNews, One Green Planet, Daily Candy, and From A to Vegan, and has been a guest on Fox 4's *Good Day* as well as numerous radio shows and podcasts, including Martha Stewart Living Radio, Our Hen House, Vegan World Radio, and the Dr. Don Show.

Find out more at TheBlissfulChef.com and visit WellnessReboot.com/blog to follow her fitness journey. You'll also find her on Twitter, Instagram, and Facebook.

BLISSFUL BITES: PLANT-BASED MEALS THAT NOURISH MIND, BODY, AND PLANET
(BenBella Books, 2011)

DEL SROUFE

Del Sroufe has worked in vegan and vegetarian kitchens for more than twenty-three years, most recently as chef and co-owner of Wellness Forum Foods, a plant-based meal delivery and catering service that emphasizes healthy, minimally processed foods. He teaches cooking classes and is the author of *Better Than Vegan* and *Forks Over Knives: The Cookbook*. He has also contributed recipes to *Food Over Medicine* by Dr. Pam Popper and Glen Merzer.

BETTER THAN VEGAN:
101 LOW-FAT, PLANT-BASED RECIPES THAT HELPED ME
LOSE OVER 200 POUNDS
(BenBella Books, 2013)

DREENA BURTON

Dreena Burton has been vegan for almost twenty years, in that time writing four best-selling cookbooks that chart her journey as a plant-powered cook and at-home mother of three. Always passionate about creating nutritious recipes, she is an advocate of using the "vegan basics" to create healthy, delicious food for the whole family. Affectionately dubbed the "Queen Bean" and "Vegan Cookie Queen" by her readers, Dreena is one of the pioneering vegan cookbook authors. Her cookbooks have garnered a loyal following, and Dreena has earned respect and repute for reliable, wholesome recipes.

Dreena graduated with distinction, receiving her Bachelor of Business Administration degree from University of New Brunswick. After working in marketing management for several years with an international satellite communications company, Dreena followed her true passion of writing recipes and cookbooks. *The Everyday Vegan* was her first project, following her father-in-law's heart attack. When the cardiologist strongly advised a low-fat, plant-based diet to her husband's parents to reverse heart disease, Dreena knew there was information needing to be shared—most importantly, how and what to eat as a vegan. After having her first child, she wrote *Vive le Vegan!*, which represented her journey as a mom and included more wholesome, easy recipes. Then came *eat, drink & be vegan*, a celebratory recipe book which has become a must-have cookbook in the vegan community and is known for its entire chapter on hummus and inventive flavor combinations. Dreena's latest cookbook, *Let Them Eat Vegan*, a whole foods vegan cookbook that is entirely wheat- and gluten-free and does not rely on vegan "subs," made the Amazon.ca best-seller list, reaching top five of all books.

Dreena has appeared on television and radio. She is a recipe contributor for well-known sites such as Kris Carr, Forks Over Knives, Engine 2 Diet, and PCRM. Dreena has written for *Yoga Journal*, *VegNews*, *ALIVE Magazine*, and has been featured in other publications including *First* magazine. She has won several blog awards, including VegNews' VegBloggy Awards and Vancouver's Ultimate Mom Blog. Her "Homestyle Chocolate Chip" video has become her signature cookie recipe and has received over 200,000 YouTube views. Dreena has strong and interactive social media communities at the following links:

WEBSITE:
plantpoweredkitchen.com
FACEBOOK:
facebook.com/DreenaBurtonPlantPoweredKitchen

TWITTER:
twitter.com/dreenaburton

HEATHER CROSBY

Heather Crosby is a T. Colin Campbell Foundation certified plant-based health coach who has developed a creative, well-loved collection of over 500 gluten-free, plant-based recipes and resources on her popular go-to website YumUniverse. In an effort to kick medication and heal herself naturally from disease, she's been fine-tuning the maintenance of this lifestyle for almost a decade, sharing what she discovers with folks who want to stay inspired.

Heather knows first-hand how overwhelming transitioning can be. It's why, in addition to YumUniverse, she continues to develop numerous resources, such as ebooks, online classes, and support groups, that have helped thousands of people not just maintain their lifestyles but thrive. Whether people are interested in this lifestyle due to environmental concerns or for better health, spiritual reasons, or love for animals, Heather proves that plant-based recipes can taste great and are fun for everyone.

YUMUNIVERSE:
INFINITE POSSIBILITIES FOR A
GLUTEN-FREE, PLANT-POWERFUL,
WHOLE-FOOD LIFESTYLE
(BenBella Books, Fall 2014)

JOHN AND MARY MCDOUGALL

John McDougall, MD, is a board-certified internist, author of twelve national best-selling books and the international online "McDougall Newsletter," host of the nationally syndicated television show *McDougall M.D.*, and medical director of the 10-day, live-in McDougall Program in Santa Rosa, CA. Other McDougall activities include seminars and health-oriented adventure vacations.

Mary McDougall is a nurse, educator, homemaker, and coauthor of eleven national best-selling books. She directs all food-oriented activities at the live-in program and has authored over 3,000 recipes for you to enjoy. She lectures nationwide on the practical methods of turning your kitchen into a health-builder for the whole family.

Previous National Best-Selling McDougall Books:

The McDougall Plan
McDougall's Medicine: A Challenging Second Opinion
The McDougall Health Supporting Cookbook, Volume 1
The McDougall Health Supporting Cookbook, Volume 2
The McDougall Plan: 12 Days to Dynamic Health
The McDougall Program for Maximum Weight Loss
The New McDougall Cookbook
The McDougall Program for Women
The McDougall Program for a Healthy Heart
The McDougall Quick and Easy Cookbook
Dr. McDougall's Digestive Tune-up
The Starch Solution

Learn more about the McDougall Program at drmcdougall.com.

LAURA THEODORE

Laura Theodore is a popular television personality and radio host, vegan chef, compassionate cookbook author, and award-winning jazz singer and actor. She is the proud creator of the Jazzy Vegetarian brand and author of *Jazzy Vegetarian: Lively Vegan Cuisine Made Easy and Delicious* and *Jazzy Vegetarian Classics: Vegan Twists on American Family Favorites.*

Laura is the on-camera host, writer, and co-producer of the *Jazzy Vegetarian* cooking show on public television. In addition, she hosts the weekly radio show, *Jazzy Vegetarian Radio*, a talk/music format focusing on plant-based recipes, eco-friendly tips, celebrity interviews, and upbeat music, served up with a bit of fun on the side.

Laura has made guest appearances on ABC, NBC, CBS, and Public Television, and she has been featured on *The Insider, Entertainment Tonight* online, News 4-NBC, Better TV, and CBS Radio. Laura has been featured in the *New York Times, USA Today, New York Daily News, New York Post, VegNews, Family Circle, Reader's Digest*, PBS Food, and *Time* magazine, among others.

As a jazz singer and songwriter, Laura has recorded six solo CDs, including her Musician Magazine Award–winning album, *Tonight's the Night.* Her CD release with the late, great Joe Beck, entitled *Golden Earrings*, was selected to appear on the 52nd Grammy Awards list in the category of Best Jazz Vocal Album. Laura has appeared in more than sixty musicals, including the hit off-Broadway show *Beehive*, which earned her a coveted Backstage Bistro Award. She was honored with the Denver Drama Critics Circle Award as Best Actress in a Musical for her starring role as Janis Joplin in the world premiere production of *Love, Janis.*

A love for good food, compassion for animals, and enthusiasm for great music has created a joyous life path for Laura Theodore.

Connect with the Jazzy Vegetarian online:

WEBSITE:
   JazzyVegetarian.com
FACEBOOK:
   facebook.com/JazzyVegetarian
TWITTER:
   twitter.com/JazzyVegetarian

JAZZY VEGETARIAN CLASSICS:
VEGAN TWISTS ON AMERICAN
FAMILY FAVORITES
(BenBella Books, 2013)

LINDSAY S. NIXON

Lindsay S. Nixon is the best-selling author of the Happy Herbivore cookbook series: *The Happy Herbivore Cookbook* (2011), *Everyday Happy Herbivore* (2011), *Happy Herbivore Abroad* (2012), and *Happy Herbivore Light & Lean* (2013). As of January 2014, Nixon has sold more than 180,000 cookbooks.

Nixon has been featured on the Food Network and *The Dr. Oz Show*, and she has spoken at Google's Pittsburgh office about health, plant-based food, and her success. Her recipes have also been featured in the *New York Times*, *Vegetarian Times* magazine, *Shape* magazine, *Bust*, *Women's Health*, WebMD, and numerous other publications. Nixon's work has also been praised and endorsed by notable leaders in the field of nutrition, including Dr. T. Colin Campbell, Dr. Caldwell B. Esselstyn Jr., Dr. Neal Barnard, Dr. John McDougall, and Dr. Pam Popper.

A rising star in the culinary world, Nixon is recognized for her ability to use everyday ingredients to create healthy, low-fat recipes that taste just as delicious as they are nutritious. For more recipes and information, visit happyherbivore.com. You can also try her 7-Day Meal Plans at getmealplans.com.

THE HAPPY HERBIVORE COOKBOOK

(BenBella Books, 2011)

EVERYDAY HAPPY HERBIVORE

(BenBella Books, 2011)

HAPPY HERBIVORE ABROAD

(BenBella Books, 2012)

HAPPY HERBIVORE LIGHT & LEAN

(BenBella Books, 2013)

TRACY RUSSELL

Tracy Russell has tried just about every fad diet and expensive "super-food" supplement out there. It wasn't until she discovered the green smoothie that she lost forty pounds, lowered her cholesterol by fifty points, and started running—marathons!

Tracy is one of the foremost experts on green smoothies and nutrition. She shares her wealth of first-hand information, research, and experiences with tens of thousands of people every day.

Tracy is the author of one of the largest green smoothie websites on the Internet, Incredible Smoothies, which she launched in 2009.

Tracy is also a contributor to *Whole Pregnancy*. She has written guest articles for other blogs and magazines as well.

THE BEST
GREEN
SMOOTHIES ON
THE PLANET
available
Fall 2014

ABOUT THE EDITOR

LeAnne Campbell, PhD, who lives in Durham, North Carolina, has been preparing meals based on a whole foods, plant-based diet for almost twenty years. LeAnne has raised two sons—Steven and Nelson, now twenty and nineteen years of age—on this diet. As a working mother, she has found ways to prepare quick and easy meals without using animal products or adding fat. She is the *New York Times* best-selling author of *The China Study Cookbook*, published by BenBella Books in 2013.

THE CHINA STUDY COOKBOOK
(BenBella Books, 2013)

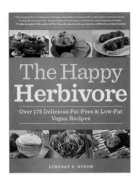

THE HAPPY HERBIVORE
COOKBOOK
(2011)

BLISSFUL BITES
(2011)

EVERYDAY HAPPY
HERBIVORE
(2011)

HAPPY HERBIVORE
ABROAD
(2012)

THE CHINA STUDY
COOKBOOK
(2013)

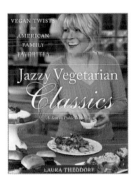

JAZZY VEGETARIAN
CLASSICS
(2013)

BETTER THAN VEGAN
(2013)

HAPPY HERBIVORE
LIGHT & LEAN
(2013)

WWW.BENBELLABOOKS.COM

CHERRY QUINOA SALAD

TRICOLORED VEGETABLE PASTA WITH SUN-DRIED MARINARA AND CASHEW CHEESE

CAULIFLOWER HOT WINGS

MEDITERRANEAN CHARD

BUDDHA LENTIL BURGER

BLUEBERRY BUNDT CAKE

WITH NEARLY 50 RECIPES FROM

The China Study Cookbook | *The Happy Herbivore series*
Better Than Vegan | *Blissful Bites*
The Best Green Smoothies on the Planet
The HappyCow Cookbook | *Jazzy Vegetarian Classics*
The PlantPure Nation Cookbook | *YumUniverse*

AND SELECTIONS FROM

Whole | *The Low-Carb Fraud*
Food Over Medicine | *Healthy Eating, Healthy World*